The Universality of
Islam

Dr. Abdallah H. Al-Kahtany

© Dr. Abdallah H. Al-Kahtany 2009
King Fahd National Library Cataloging in-Publication Data

Al-Kahtany, Abdallah H

The Universality of Islam

ISBN: 9960-9135-4-6
1 - Islam - General principles   1 - Title

L.D. No. 3053/21
ISBN: 9960-9135-4-6

ISBN: 9960-9441-5-8

Cover Design & Layout by C.P. Muneer Ahmed, Kerala, India

O Mankind! We have created you from male and female and made you nations and tribes that you may appreciate one another Indeed, the most noble of you in the Sight of Allah is the most righteous [i.e., conscious of his]. Indeed, Allah is knowing and [all] Acquainted.

(The Qur'an 49:13)

CONTENTS

FOREWORD

By the generosity of The Merciful, three different editions of the **Universality of Islam** have travelled worldwide. Readers had varying opinions towards it: some took the liberty of copying whole chapters in their website; others expressed their attitudes, critiques, and comments to me in person or in writing; and few expressed their displeasure and disagreement with it. My firm understanding of our human nature helped me to understand such varying attitudes. However, among the numerous responses to the **Universality of Islam,** no one questioned its originality and methodology. I am very thankful to all those who took the time to analyze its arguments and propositions regardless of what they think of it.

I am tremendously thankful to Allah, The Omnipotent, for granting me the opportunity to extensively revise and publish this fourth edition of the **Universality of Islam** after more than a decade since the appearance of the first edition. I benefited greatly from the numerous comments, suggestions and corrections I have been receiving over the years. Some thing I always had in mind since the first time I thought of writing a book about the universality of Islam was the responsibility of handling this topic with utmost sincerity and objectivity. Nonetheless, any critiques, comments, suggestions and reviews will be welcomed. I am only a humble human being trying his best to contribute in clarifying some of the critical issues of universality in the era of globalization. Issues that I think we need to ponder upon with seriousness and open-mindedness.

It is my greatest pleasure to receive respected readers' comments, corrections and suggestions at the following addresses:

Address of the author:
Abdallah H. Al-Kahtany
P.O. Box 9012
King Khalid University
Abha, Saudi Arabia
E-mail: aalkahtany@gmail.com

ACKNOWLEDGEMENTS

"Those who do not thank people do not thank Allah." Gratefulness is a prophetic tradition; humanity at large needs to observe. Many are those who contributed to the emergence of this book and hence deserve the best of thanks. Among those who contributed significantly to the completion of this book are:

- Dr. Abdallah Ali Abu Ishi's encouragement and brotherly support was very motivating and inspiring.

- My late brother Dr. Abdulrahman Al-Jamhoor's death did not spare him to see this edition of a book he adored and supported greatly. May Allah shower him with His mercy.

- The two anonymous reviewers'-appointed by al-Muntada Al-Islami in London- comments and suggestions on an earlier edition were very constructive.

- Professor William L. Tarvin's and Razik Sammander's reviews of the earlier scripts were very helpful.

- The respected sister, Mrs. Samira Van Fossen (Om Mohamed), deserves the utmost thanks and sincerest du'a for her very accurate corrections and suggestions that reflected in-depth understanding and keen interest in the topic.

- Dr. Iejaz M. Sheikh encouraging comments and suggestions were very valuable.

- My dear parents unlimited support, sincere supplications, overwhelming love and sacrifices can never be rewarded but by Allah, The Merciful.

- My wife's and children's forbearance and sacrifice during the compilation of this book can never be forgotten.

- You as a respected reader who gave my words honor by taking some of their valuable time to read them.

INTRODUCTION

In the 21st century, means of communication and transportation have gone beyond all expectations and cross-cultural awareness has become widespread. After the collapse of communism and consequently the Soviet Union and many other communist countries, proposals were presented urging the adoption of universal laws, values and morals with which relationships among the peoples of the world should be governed.

Recently, the idea of a so-called New World Order was proposed through the United Nations in order to prescribe values and impose laws on peoples of various cultures. The question that will immediately emerge is whose values, laws and ways of life should be adopted? Because the United States is, presently, the 'only superpower' among all the nations of the world, as well as the largest financial contributor to the United Nations, it seems a forgone conclusion that the American way of life will be the only choice presented to the globe. Charles Krauthammer, an influential American columnist, wrote in **The Foreign Affairs** that a uni-polar moment had arrived and that a confident United States should learn to accept its new role, aggressively imposing its own vision.[1]

Given the natural richness and military power of the U.S., why have its values not provided happiness and peace of mind to the millions of Americans whose lives have been wrecked by alcoholism, violence, drug use and other family and social dilemmas? Can such a way of life that has failed to uproot discrimination against blacks and other minorities bring equality among the social castes of India? Can the American way of life that has resulted in grave failure when attempting to solve the problem of homelessness, provide solutions to the problems of poverty in South America or Africa? Such questions should be raised against V. S. Naipaul's claim that western civilization is the universal civilization that fits all men. David Gergen, editor at large of U.S. News & World Report has candidly uttered his doubts:

> The United States cannot achieve order in
> its streets or even in its capital, much less
> in the rest of the world.[2]

Some might say that the New World Order does not have to be that of the Americans; it could be that of the British, the French, the Russians or the Chinese; all are permanent members of the Security Council. Nevertheless, these governments have never claimed to bring happiness nor security to their own nations or the rest of the world. Nonetheless, no nation in the whole world would willingly

---

1 - David Gergen. American Missed Opportunities. **Foreign Affairs,** 1993, p.1.
2 - Gergen, 1993, p.1.

choose or suggest a way of life detrimental to their own interests. Any system of life selected as the basis for a New World Order is almost certain to serve the interests of the people proposing and sponsoring it. People can only adhere willingly and peacefully to a system of their choice.

Gergen (1993) shows the level of self-interest felt by the people of the world's most dominant country regarding their care for other nations:

> The American public told pollsters from the Chicago Council on Foreign Relations that the most important priorities of U.S. foreign policy should be, first, protecting jobs of American workers; second, protecting the interest of American workers abroad; and third, securing adequate supplies of energy. Defending allies, preventing the spread of nuclear weapons and advancing human rights were seen as less important. Helping to spread democracy to other nations was 15th on list of 15 priorities.[3]

Samuel Huntington refers to the standards western nations apply to their interests in the world:

> The West in effect is using international institutions, military power and economic resources to run the world in ways that will maintain Western predominance protect Western interests and promote Western political and economical values[4.]

Accepting these New Order premises as a way of life

---

3 - Gergen. 1993.
4 - Samuel Huntington. Clash of Civilizations. **The Foreign Affairs**, Summer 1993.

means full submission to the teachings and rules that such a system puts forward. Naturally, the result of such acceptance is a materialistic and secular view of life.

The probability that such a New World Order will be accepted or applied is extremely remote. It has as much chance as such old world orders as colonialism, communism, dark ages theology, and modern capitalism.

The well-known American writer and senior advisor to three American presidents, Patrick J. Buchanan, thinks that demanding that the Muslim world, with its great cultural and moral treasures, should accept the western ideology is the 'irony of ironies'. He writes:

> Today, an aging, dying Christian West is pressing the Third World and the Islamic world to accept contraception, abortion, and sterilization as the West has done. But why should they enter a suicide pact with us when they stand to inherit the earth when we are gone?[5]

There is a dire need among the majority of the world's population for a way of life that can solve their problems and answer their unanswered questions about existence and destiny. With escalating rates of immorality and violence in the world, increasing numbers of people have been searching for a way out. Many have found suicide to be the easiest and probably fastest solution. No wonder our world is wading in a state of chaos. It has tried so many ideologies and applied countless socioeconomic theories, but none have proven to be quite right. That which has been tried has failed, and that which has failed has been tried again . . . and again. Surely the time has come to ask questions if there is another way, an alternative system that could be adopted by

5 - Patrick J. Buchanan, The Death of the West. St. Martin's Press: New York, 2002, p. 48.

the whole world.

Nominating a system to bind the people of all nations into one nation is a serious undertaking. It is imperative that everyone's freedom of choice is safeguarded and that their inherent beliefs and concerns are respected. Any universal doctrine, law, system or way of life should take into consideration the natural characteristics of humankind. Such a system should have the following attributes among its major principles:

1. Non-Discriminatory:

> It should emphasize equality and reject all types of racism and discrimination. Its basic teachings and values should be stable and should be equally and justly applied to all people with no discrimination because of their color, ethnicity, etc.

2. Tolerant:

> It should tolerate the existence of difference in belief, language, and cultural diversity among peoples of the world.

3.   Ethically progressive:

> It should not oppose advancements in science and technology, but rather provide universal ethics to ensure the consequences of such advancements are positive.

4.   Provide working solutions to pressing problems:

> It should provide solutions to humanity's problems such as: alcoholism, drug addiction, the break down of family and social systems, unrestrained sexuality, rape, and the abuse and molestation of women and children.

The beauty of Islam as the only universal alternative way of life for humanity has been misrepresented by some of the un-islamic malpractices by some Muslims and the misconceptions brought up by people of little knowledge about Islam or through prejudiced views. Terrorist activities launched by a very insignificant minority in the name of Islam is unjustly blamed on the over a billion Muslims who have never approved of them. They themselves suffer such irrational and irresponsible actions.

In the following chapters of this book, Islamic principles of equality, tolerance, solutions to problems facing humanity and position towards sciences and advancements will be compared to a number of contemporary ideologies and religions that may aspire for universality. The last chapter concludes with some of the major inherent principles of Islam as part and parcel of its teachings for the betterment of humanity.   ●

CHAPTER I
Universality and Equality

The principle of equality in dealing with people of different colors, socioeconomic status and cultures is absent from the dominant ideologies of today's world. Indian society has suffered from a rigidly applied caste system for many centuries: some people are looked at as gods (avatars), while others are treated little better than slaves.

Although Christianity has seldom been applied as a system for living, it contains, among its contemporary teachings doctrines that can be viewed as discriminatory. The Talmud (the basis of contemporary Judaism) considers the Jews to be privileged over all other people (the Gentiles).

The list could be expanded to include the communist slogan of equality-all people are equal- then never practiced, which, in reality, means that some are more equal than others. Capitalism, as applied in several Western societies, is

The communist slogan of equality-all people are equal- never practiced, which, in reality, means that some are more equal than others. Capitalism, as applied in several Western societies, is not geared theoretically to establishing equality, since it encourages division between the rich and the poor. Socialism, which in theory is supposed to ameliorate the excesses of capitalism and communism, successfully highlighted the inherent weakness of communism and capitalism.

not geared theoretically to establishing equality, since it encourages division between the rich and the poor. Socialism, which in theory is supposed to ameliorate the excesses of capitalism and communism, successfully highlighted the inherent weakness of communism and capitalism. Yet, could not prove itself as a more viable alternative.

Of all the existing ideological systems, only Islam remains the only option that appeals to all because it respects the rights of all people and regards all humans as members of one nation living under God (Allah), in peace and harmony, in spite of their many differences. Historical and contemporary evidence stand as witness to the non-negotiable Islamic equality.

1. Christianity and Equality

In this section, I will examine some of the teachings of Christianity in order to determine if such views could appeal to all people regardless of their differences. To be objective, reference will be made to the book of Christianity, The Bible, to document whether the message of Christ (pbuh) was for the world or limited in time and space to his people, the Israelites. Hence, it does not have a universal appeal.

According to Matthew, the message Jesus (pbuh) received was limited to one nation. Jesus (pbuh) stated clearly in his instructions to his disciples that they were not to spread the message beyond the tribes of Israel.

> Go not into the way of the gentiles, and into any town of the Samaritans enter ye not: but go rather to the lost sheep of the house of Israel .....[6]   (Matthew 10:5, 6)

Another incident narrated about Jesus (pbuh) further illustrates the point in question:[7]

> Leaving that place, Jesus withdrew to the region of Tyre and Sidon. A Canaanite woman from that vicinity came to him, crying out, Lord, Son of David, have mercy on me! My daughter is suffering terribly from demon's possession. Jesus did not answer a word. So his disciples came to him and urged him, send her away, for she keeps crying out after us.
> He answered, I was sent only to the lost sheep of Israel.
> The woman came and knelt before him. Lord, help me! she said.
> He replied, it is not right to take the children's bread and toss it to their dogs.

---

6 - Quotes were taken form **The Holy Bible** The Gideon's International in the British Isles, Western House,George Street, Luttersorth, Leics, LE17 4EE.
7- Matthew 15:24

(Matthew 15: 21 - 26).

In these biblical excerpts, Jesus (pbuh) has clearly stated that his message was to be spread among the people of Israel only and, not to the people of all nations. However, as a Muslim who believes that Jesus Christ (pbuh) was a great Messenger of Allah, I am convinced that Jesus never said the underlined quote from the Bible (Matthew 15:26).

Hill and Cheadle (1996) mentioned that colored people have been mistreated through out the history of people of European descendants. "Western European tradition has generally segregated blacks and throughout history, moving their roles and contributions into the background or omitting them completely"[8].

Though the prophets of God can never preach hatred or discriminations, the continuous additions to the Bible by different groups to manipulate its teachings for their own interests, some passages denote discriminatory sense.

And Mariam and Aaron spoke against
Moses because of the Ethiopian woman
whom he had married: for he had married
an Ethiopian woman (Numbers 12:1).

Such excerpts from the Old Testament might explain the discriminatory treatment against the Jews of an African origin in the State of Israel. The feeling of discrimination among the African Christian American led to the reactionary feeling of some predominant Afro-American Clergy. On Good Friday, 1993, Archbishop George Augustus Stallings, Jr. of Washington D.C., burned an image of a white Jesus in the street as he proclaimed its "historical inaccuracy": "Jesus was an 'Afro-Asiatic Jew'."[9] To realize the extent the level of

---

8 - Jim Hill and Rand Cheadle. **The Bible Tells Me So**. Anchor Books/ Doubleday: New York, 1996, p. 13.
9 - Hill and Cheadle, p.13.

The Jewish lobby is very powerful and plays a very effective role in shaping US foreign policy; especially those in Israel's interest.

racism in the world's most powerful country, there are around 327 white supremacy groups in the U.S.[10]

2. The Jewish Position Towards Other Nations.

As we will see in this section, the true unashamedly discriminatory nature of Judaism means that it cannot be nominated as a universal system for all humankind to follow. Despite its nature or perhaps even because of it- the Jewish lobby is very powerful and plays a very effective role in shaping US foreign policy; especially those in Israel's interest.

The Jewish book of guidance, the Talmud, the preeminent authority for the Jews,[11] ranks them above all other people. Jews are considered to be the chosen people of God. They are supreme, and the multitude gentile (non-Jewish) surrounding them are considered

---

10 - Hill and Cheadle, p.12.
11 - The modern Jewish writer Herman Wouk states very clearly in his book; **This is My God** that: "The Talmud is to this day the circulating heart's blood of the Jewish religion. Whatever we are, Orthodox, Conservative, Reform or merely spasmodic sentimentalists, we follow the Talmud. It is our common law." This statement was presented by T. Pike in his book **Israel Our Duty. . Our Dilemma**. 1984, P. 54.

unclean and sub-humans.

The reason that Jews claim selected by God and the gentiles as unclean is that the Jews were present at Mt. Sinai, but gentiles were not.[12]

> When the serpent came into Eve he infused filthy lust into her . . . . When Israel stood in Sinai that lust was eliminated, but the lust of idolaters, who did not stand on Sinai, did not cease (Abodah Zarah 22b).[13]

Let's look in the Zohar, where the Jewish rabbis interpreted the verse from Genesis: "Now the serpent is more subtle than any beast of the field". Their interpretation is:

> More subtle that is towards evil; than all the beasts, that is, the idolatrous people of the earth. For they are the children of the ancient serpent which seduced Eve.
> (Zohar 1: 28b)

As a matter of fact, non-Jews (gentiles), whether Christians, Buddhists or Hindus are not considered equal to the Jews in any way; the Jewish doctrine regards them as if they were non-humans. The following excerpt from the Talmud would make any one puzzle over the way they disparage other people:

> A gentile … is not a neighbor in the sense of reciprocating and being responsible for damages caused by his negligence; nor does he watch over his cattle. Even the best gentile laws were too crude to admit of reciprocity. (Bek. 13b)

---

12 - References to the Talmudic verses were taken from the Talmudic authority Rev. Theodore W. Pike. in his book **Israel Our Duty .. Our Dilemma. Big Sky** Press, 1984.

13 - Compare with what the Qur'an says about Adam and Eve in 7: 19-25.

See how this conflicts with the true sense of justice in the Qur'an:

> O ye who believe! Stand out firmly for Allah, witness in justice, and let not the hatred of others make you depart from justice. Be just: That is nearer to piety. And fear Allah, for Allah is well-acquainted with all that you do.   (Qur'an 5: 8)

Christians and other non-Jews (called heathens in the Talmud) were not exempted from the hatred and the distrust of Jews:

> Where a suit arises between an Israelite and a heathen, if you can satisfy the former according to the laws of Israel, justify him and say: This is our law; so also if you can justify him by the law of the heathens justify him and say (to the other party): This is your law; but if this can't be done, we use subterfuges to circumvent them. (Baba Kama 113 a)

The Jewish Encyclopedia summarizes opinions of the sages about this law by stating:

> The Mishnah . . . declares that if a gentile sues an Israelite, the verdict is for the defendant; if the Israelite is the plaintiff, he obtains full damages.[14]

There are numerous citations in the Talmud where non-Jews are considered dirty or unworthy of living. It goes to the extent that such people are not even worthy of being accepted in their religion, even if they so desired. In fact, the Talmud prohibits, under the threat of death, the teaching of

---

14 - **The Jewish Encyclopedia**. ed. Cyrus Adler, Isidore Singer. New York, London: Funk-Wagnalls, 1901-1906. P. 620.

The occupying Zionist policies against the Palestinians reveals the real nature of the extreme brutality and hatred they have against children, women and helpless old people.

the Torah to any gentile:

> Hence the Talmud prohibited the teaching to a Gentile of the Torah, the inheritance of the congregation of Jacob R. Johannan declares if one dared to do so such a person deserves death.[15]

Certainly such a system, with its extreme discriminatory nature, was not designed to be *a universal way of life*.

Many Israeli leaders do not value the lives of non-Jewish people. Menachem Begin's response to the world outrage over massacres in Sabra and Shatilla refugee camps in Lebanon is reflective of this attitude:

> Goyim [meaning gentiles] are killing Goyim and they came to hang the Jews.[16]

Some might say that current Judaism is not built on such radical or racial ideas. Let's listen to the defense of the leading Israeli authority as to what they have done in Leba-

---

15- T. Pike, cited on page 61 that this information is cited fromThe Jewish Encyclopedia., Article, Gentile, p. 623, where the reference is Sanh. 59a, Hagigah 13a.
16 - T. Pike, P. 53.

non. One is really stunned by the Talmudic manner in which they spoke. An example of this was seen in the way Begin arrogantly informed the Americans about the massacre he had committed:

> We have no duty to explain our actions to
> others - only to ourselves.[17]

In other words, the Jew is above criticism by a gentile.

Observing the occupying Zionist policies against the Palestinians reveals the real nature of the extreme brutality and hatred they have against children, women and helpless old people. Israeli officials have become candid in their rejection of the gentile's law when not favoring the Jews. After the decision by the International Court of Justice that construction of the partition wall was against the international law, Yousef Lapid, Israel's justice minister, told the state-controlled radio on July 10th, 2004 that Israel would pay attention to the ruling of the Hague-based ICJ: "We will heed the ruling of our supreme court, not the ruling of ICJ". This is the typical Talmudic Zionist view of contempt for everything non-Jewish. The whole world is always wrong, the tens of UN resolutions condemning Israel are not fair, the many bloody and inhuman massacres in Palestinian camps are just for self-defense, bombing UN-run refugee camps and killing indiscriminately is a Zionist right. Mistreating and even constant killings of journalists and peace activists are just unintended mistakes, etc.

This attitude is not confined to politicians. Moshe Antelman of Rehovot, Israel - a rabbi and a chemist - developed a bullet containing pork fat.

Antelman, a rabbi and a chemist,

---

17 - T. Pike , P. 72. For more information about Jewish atrocities look at the New York Times, August 5,1985, P.1, and The National Geographic, April 1983, P. 514.

developed the lard-laden ammo for use against devout Muslims, who believe any contact with pig flesh robs the soul of its chance to enter paradise. . .[18] The good rabbi has offered his innovation to West Bank settlers, and he also hopes to interest the Pentagon in this refined form of military pork.[19]

This is just one example of how the Jewish elite and leaders value people of other nations.

The Zionist nature of hatred for other nations and the

---

18 - This is not true. Muslims are only forbidden from eating pork. According to the Old Testament, consumption of pork is forbidden: (Leviticus 11: 7-8)

19 - **Sunday**. August 28, 1994, P. 18.

The whole world is always wrong, the tens of UN resolutions condemning Israel are not fair, the many bloody and inhuman massacres in Palestinian camps are just for self-defense, bombing UN-run refugee camps and killing indiscriminately is a Zionist right. Mistreating and even constant killings of journalists and peace activists are just unintended mistakes.

complex sense of superiority have led them to direct their guns to their closest allies (the Americans) and killed many soldiers; as exemplified by their savage attack on the American navy ship 'Liberty', in midday.[20]

In an interview with the prominent Jewish American thinker and MIT linguist, Prof. Noam Chomsky, responded to a question about the Jewish view of other people by saying:

> If you go back to traditional Jewish culture in either Eastern Europe or North Africa, being a Christian, a non-Jew, was a different species, below the level of Jews. For example, Jewish doctors are not supposed to treat non-Jews unless Jews can gain by it. So Maimonides[21] could be the doctor for the Sultan because Jews would gain by it, but not otherwise.

When the following question was addressed to Chomsky;

> "Is this canonical or a cultural tradition?" He said:
> It's in the Halakah, the rabbinic tradition. There's plenty of stuff like this. They (the Jews) were on the one hand an oppressed minority, but on the other hand very racist. The racism carried over when they became a non-oppressed majority.[22]

The preceding section focused on the Jewish view of other nations. The author depended heavily on Judaic

---

20 - For more details see Paul Findley's book **They Dare to Speak**, published in first in 1985 by Lawrence Hill Books, pp (165- 179).
21 - Refers to Sultan Salaahudeen's (Saldin) Jewish physician.
22 - David Barsamian and Noam Chomsky . **Propaganda and the Public Mind.** South End Press: Cambridge. 2001, p. 85.

sources that have left doubt that discriminating against other people was an ideological and a religious duty of Zionist Jews. Since Jewish-ness is only inherited, other people of any nation can never be part of it. Other people are excluded and can never be part of that narrow system that favors Jews over all other nations, for no reason but because they are Jews.

3. The Socio-Religious System of Hinduism

In this section, we will see that just as its racist doctrines exclude Judaism from being nominated as a candidate for the universal way of life, so too does Hinduism eliminate itself from consideration for precisely the same reason- racism. Hinduism is built around a racist apparatus incorporating a discriminatory caste system, which is an integral part of this religion. The caste system divides Hindu society into four major groups:

Hinduism is built around a racist apparatus incorporating a discriminatory caste system, which is an integral part of this religion.

a. The Brahmans: the learned and the priestly class.
b. The Kashattriyas: the fighting and ruling class.
c. The Vaisyas: the trading and the agricultural people.
d. The Suddras: the lowest caste whose only business is to serve their superiors.[23]

And the Dalits or the Untouchables who are outcaste

---

23 - Gustave le Bon. Les Civilization de lInde. P. 211.

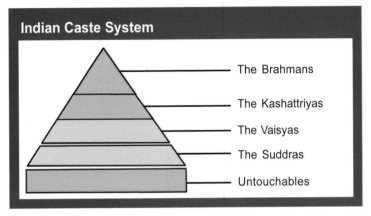

Indian Caste System

- The Brahmans
- The Kashattriyas
- The Vaisyas
- The Suddras
- Untouchables

because they do not belong to any of the original fourfold grouping. They are untouchable because their touch is bond to pollute the other castes. Thus, they must remain at a sufficient distance from the other castes. These groups are only the head of the very complicated social fabric of the Hindu society, which contains about 2800 unique communities.[24]

These castes are worlds apart from each other. This is one of the most outrageous manifestations of inequality now being practiced anywhere. One is born in one caste and dies in that caste. It is one, which even the present political system of India repudiates.

This system was incorporated into the teachings of Hinduism during the time of Manu, during the heydays of the Brahman civilization. Since then, it has become an integral part of the Hindu socioreligious system. It has become more or less a hereditary system, subjugating the majority of the population, and is exploited by the minority ruling class to

---

24 - John Campbell Oman, The Brahmans, Theists and Muslims of India. Delhi, 1973, p.50, and Dalit Voice, 15:4, p.20. In Fazlie, 1997,p.148-9.

The caste system is not a thing of the past, but also it has its manifestations on present day politics.

maintain its purity and superiority.

Gustave le Bon mentioned some of Manu's (One of the major authors of the Hindu teachings, the Vedas) teachings:
This law gave to the Brahmans the distinction, superiority and sanctity, which raised their status, equal to that of the gods . . . Anyone who is born a Brahman is the noblest creature on earth. He is the monarch of all the created things and his duty is to defend the Shastras, the Hindu teachings that provides legitimacy to their power.[25]

Manu goes on to grant more rights to the Brahmans at the expanse of all other people:
Whatever is on the earth belongs to the Brahman, for he is the highest among all creatures. All things are for him.[26]

The Sudras have no rights whatsoever in Hindu society. They are considered lower than the animals.
A Sudra should never acquire property, even if he has the opportunity, for in so doing he is causing pain to the Brahmans. Nothing can be more honorable for a Sudra

---

25 - Ibid., P. 211.
26 - Ibid., P. 211.

> than to serve the Brahman; nothing
> besides this can earn him any reward . . .
> A Sudra who assaults a higher-caste man
> is liable to lose the limb with which the
> assault is made . . . [27]
> And so it goes on, unceasingly
> condescending:
> The atonement for killing a dog, a cat, a
> frog, a lizard, a crow, an owl and a Sudra
> is the same.[28]

This extremely discriminatory system is not a thing of the past, but also it has its manifestations on present day politics. It would be extremely difficult to believe, accept or adopt such an unjust system as a way of life, not to mention a global system for humanity.

4. Capitalism

Capitalism is not a religion but it has become a way of life that millions of people aspire to and once achieved, defend with great enthusiasm. Millions of people have been fooled by the symbols of American capitalism,[29] such as the Statue of Liberty welcoming every newcomer to the land of happiness and opportunity. However, it seems as if many people have forgotten the history of slavery, the plantations, and the back-of-the-bus theory where blacks were not allowed to sit in the front seats of public transportation.

Few capitalists seem bothered by the dire consequences of the unbridled pursuit of possessions and wealth such as: escalating rates of crime, rape, child molestation, battered women, drug addiction, covert and overt discrimination, homelessness, and the calamity facing old people.

---

27 - Ibid., P. 211.
28 - Ibid., P. 212.
29 - Ibid., P. 212.

ENJOY
Capitalism

Capitalism is not a religion but it has become a way of life that millions of people aspire to and once achieved, defend with great enthusiasm. Millions of people have been fooled by the symbols of American capitalism, such as the Statue of Liberty welcoming every newcomer to the land of happiness and opportunity.

As a result of unequal treatment and discrimination, the Afro-American community is facing a number of escalating problems. White America faces the same problems, but the alarming difference is of scale.

Phillipson (1992) referred to the key investigator for Phelps-Stokes Fund, Thomas Jesse Jones, a Welsh American who was closely associated with the policy of separate education for the blacks of the USA. The philosophy behind the policy of providing appropriate education for the blacks was formulated clearly at the turn of the century on purely discriminatory grounds. The black people were viewed as a lower race fit for lower education and good for humble jobs because they were not white:

the white people are to be the leaders ... the Caucasian will rule ... in the negro is the opportunity of the South. Time has proven that he is best fitted to perform the heavy labor in the Southern states ... He will willingly fill the more menial positions, and do the heavy work, at less wages, than the American white man or any foreign race" (quoted in Berman 1982: 180 and cited in Phillipson 1992: 199).[30]

Sixty-nine percent of all births of the African-American community are out of wedlock. Two thirds of their children live in single parent homes. About one third of Afro-American boys can expect to serve a jail or prison sentence before the age of sixteen. Four out of ten black males aged sixteen to thirty-five are in jail, in prison, on parole, or are on probation. The highest rates of drug consumption, school dropouts and rape are found also among blacks.[31] Buchanan referred to this and similar statistics regarding minorities in an accusatory manner rather than trying to find out the real reasons behind such alarming statistics. Minorities that in the past faced slavery and extreme forms of brutality and discrimination are now experiencing covert institutional negligence and discrimination. Little effort to restore equality and justice is evident. Making retribution for the evil centuries and shameful history is studiously avoided, but pinpointing fingers and blaming the oppressed is not. An unsuitable system at the local level can never meet the challenges of a complicated and diverse world.

---

30 - Robert Phillipson. Linguistic Imperialism. (Oxford University Press, 1992), 119.
31 - **William J. Bennett,** Index of Leading Cultural Indicators. **(New York: Broadway Books, 2000), pp. 50, 27.**

Basically, Capitalism results in economic inequality, particularly for minorities and 'non-producing segments', such as children and the elderly. Because of the great changes that have taken place in America and other western societies during the last one hundred years, many social problems have emerged. The huge corporate invasion of family farms and small family-centered enterprises have resulted in many socioeconomic tensions. Although the capitalist system as a way of life has provided material gains for a small number of individuals, large segments of society suffer: among them the senior citizens, single women, children born out of wedlock, and the non-white minorities.

A common sight in downtown areas of American cities is the many elderly people among the homeless. A number of American sociologists forecast that the problems faced by the elderly will become even more severe in the near future.[32] Declining birthrates and increasing numbers of elderly people indicate that such trends will continue. It is expected that the elderly will soon constitute a large proportion of society. In 1900, people over 65 constituted four percent of the American population (three million people); by 1976, they comprised over 10 percent of the populace (22 million). It is projected that by 2030 there will be more than 50 million people over 65 in the United States - making about 17 percent of the population.[33] This is not just an American

---

32 - **Sullivan, Thompson, Wright, Gross and Spady (1980) in their book** Social Problems: Divergent Perspectives. **(John Wiley & Sons, New York), discuss the great changes in the Socioeconomic life of Americans:** The social status of the elderly has declined because they no longer hold positions of economic power; their children are no longer dependent on them for their own livelihood; and they no longer perform tasks that are viewed as essential for the group's welfare (P. 340).

33 - **According to the American Institute of Gerontology,** Information on Aging **(Wayne State University / University of Michigan, no. 10, October 1,1976).**

problem, it is a capitalist problem caused because individual wealth is valued over all things, including people. According to the UN statistics on the depopulation of capitalist Europe, in the year 2000, there were 494 million Europeans aged fifteen to sixty-five. That is projected to plunge to 365 million by 2050; however, the 107 million Europeans over sixty-five today will soar to 172 million in the same period.[34] By that time, more than a third of Europe's people will be over sixty.

Western nations believe that their civilization and culture are superior, and that they have the right to impose their rule and way of life on "inferior" civilizations, cultures and peoples.

Regardless of the miserable treatment that the elderly, the poor and the colored face in the form of covert and overt discrimination, western nations believe that their civilization and culture are superior, and that they have the right to impose their rule and way of life on "inferior" civilizations, cultures and peoples.

Capitalism, in theory, calls for an equal treatment be-

---

34 - **Population Division, Department of Economics and Social Affairs, United Nations Secretariat,** Replacement Migration: Is It a Solution to Declining and Aging Population? **March 21, 2000, p139. In P. J. Buchanan .** Death of the West. **St. Martin's Press: New York. pp. 97-8**

The dignity of the human has to be restored through a universal way of life that is not discriminatory and that views man the most dignified creature on earth. This will lead us to our final destination in search of the only universal system of life.

tween all the segments of society; in practice it can never provide the right mechanism to do so. It institutes a different type of rigid socio-economic castes, which result in segregation and unequal access to social, health and educational services. The rights of the strong sectors of society are preserved- the young, the rich, the white, etc- while the rights of the weak sectors -women, children, elderly people, single parents, elderly people, etc. - are overlooked.

There is no point in discussing the topic of equality and communism here, since it has been discredited and abandoned by most of its own theoreticians and practitioners, regardless of all rigorous modifications. It brought little or no good to the nations that have adopted it at the point of the gun: only the ills of poverty, backwardness and misery.

Capitalism is rooted in monopoly, the rich becomes richer while the poor gets poorer; otherwise, there will be no capitalism. The world is not in need for more global economical exploitations at the hands of the multinational capitalist company. The dignity of the human has to be restored through a universal way of life that is not discriminatory and that views man the most dignified creature on earth. This will lead us to our final destination in search of the only universal system of life, which is mankind's only hope for a nondiscriminatory treatment.

5. Islam and Universal Equality

Any system that assumes universal applicability should appreciate its followers' potentials and recognize their achievements, regardless of their ethnic, racial, geographical or socioeconomic backgrounds. In other words, such a system should only evaluate their potential (or their accomplishment), and not what they have naturally been endowed with in terms of such as, their color, race, country of origin, etc. Islam views people as equal. In fact, in Islam inherent differences have a greater wisdom that is worthy of appreciation. The religion, which views that all people are equal in the eyes of their Creator, is Islam:

> And of His signs is the creation of the heavens and the earth, and the diversity of your languages and colors. Indeed, in that are signs for those of knowledge.
>
> (The Qur'an 30:22)
>
> Prophet Muhammad (pbuh) said: No Arab has any superiority over a non-Arab, nor does a white man have any superiority over a black man, or the black man any superiority over the white man. You are all the children of Adam, and Adam was created from dust/earth.[35]

Islam rejects all forms of superiority complex based

---

35 - Narrated by Bayhaqi and Bazzaar.

Prophet Muhammad (pbuh) said: No Arab has any superiority over a non-Arab, nor does a white man have any superiority over a black man, or the black man any superiority over the white man. You are all the children of Adam, and Adam was created from dust/earth.

on racial, geographical, economical, linguistic or other inherent factors. It considers righteousness and good conduct as the basis for recognition. In relation to this principle, Allah The Almighty says:

> O Mankind! We have created you from male and female and made you nations and tribes that you may appreciate one another. Indeed, the most noble of you in the Sight of Allah is the most righteous [i.e., conscious of him]. Indeed, Allah is knowing and [all] Acquainted.

(The Qur'an 49:13)

On the Plains of Arafat more than fourteen hundred years ago, Prophet Mohammed (pbuh) declared the Islamic eternal principles of equality to a gathering of more than one hundred thousand. Therefore, every listener would pass what he had heard to those who were not present:

O. People! Your Lord is one. Your father is

one. All of you came from Adam and Adam was created from dust. The noblest among you before Allah is the most righteous. No Arab has any superiority over a non-Arab, nor does a non-Arab over an Arab. A white man has no superiority over a black man, nor does a black man over a white man but with righteousness. Have I clearly conveyed the message? O. Allah you are the Witness. Let the one who is present deliver the message to the absent ones.

Prof. Ramakrishna Rao, a professing Hindu,[36] quoted Sarojini Naidu, the greatest Indian poetess, who spoke about how equality has been practiced in Islam by saying:

It was the first religion that preached and practiced democracy; for, in the mosque, when the adhan (the Muslim call to prayer) is sounded and the worshippers are gathered together, the equality of Islam is embodied five times a day when the peasant and the king kneel side by side and proclaim, God alone is great.

The great poetess of India continues:

I have been struck over and again by this indivisible unity of Islam that makes a man instinctively a brother. When you meet an Egyptian, an Algerian, an Indian and a Turk in London, Egypt is the motherland for one and India is the motherland for another.[37]

---

36 - Professor of Philosophy, University of Mysore, India.
37 - **K.S. Ramakrishna Rao.** Mohammad: The Prophet of Islam. **Al-Furqan Agency. P. 11.**

Equality as an uncompromised Islamic principle is not recognized as a mere slogan to aspire for. It is practiced on a daily basis through the five daily prayers, where Muslims submit to God standing on straight lines with no distinction between them. The ultimate universal nature of Islam is exemplified during the Hajj (Pilgrimage) where about three million Muslims from more than 70 countries gather in one place with the same dress for the sake of pleasing God and glorifying Him. All barriers including that of race, color, language and status collapse.

As some systems promote religious exclusiveness and discrimination (Judaism, Hinduism, Christianity) and yet others encourage economic; consequently social, inequality (capitalism, communism and socialism), only Islam is an all-embracing and equalitarian system. This leads us to a second comparison between Islam and other existing ideological systems in relation to tolerance, the second condition for any proposed World Order. ●

Any system, which claims universality, should have tolerance towards other cultural and religious practices as a non-negotiable principle.

CHAPTER II

Universality and Tolerance

If there is a unique attribute that our world has, it is diversity in both culture and belief. Therefore, any system, which claims universality, should have tolerance towards other cultural and religious practices as a non-negotiable principle. In this section of the book, light will be shed on the principle of tolerance based on historical evidence drawn from practices of several religions and ideologies in comparison to Islam. Since the previous section revealed the exclusive basis of Jewish intolerance, I will begin with Christianity, which some believe manifests the kindness and gentility of Christ (pbuh). But when we apply an historical examination, the conclusion is completely the opposite. Regardless of the teachings of Christianity and Judaism that started at the hand of the most tolerant among people, the prophets of Allah, a lot has emerged which can never be part of their teachings but added over the ages.

1. The Crusaders' Behavior in Palestine

Let's look at what the Christian Crusaders did to the Muslims when they waged wars against them and when they occupied Jerusalem. These wars were referred to as The Holy Wars, which were conducted with the blessings of the Pope and under the banner of the Christian religious leaders.

Although Jerusalem was surrounded for more than a month, its inhabitants resisted the Crusaders' invasion courageously. When the Crusaders finally won, they rushed through the streets killing, destroying and burning whatever they saw in their way. They did not differentiate between men, women or children. The massacre lasted for the whole night. On Friday, 15th of June 1099, the Crusaders stormed the gates of Al-Aqsaa Mosque and killed all those who were taking refuge inside it. Ibn Al-Atheer described the massacre in his book Al-Kamil as follows:

> The Crusaders killed more than 70 thousand people. Some of those who were killed were Muslim scholars, erudites and adorationists who left their countries to dwell near the holy places. They stole more than 40 silver lanterns from the Holy Rock, each costing at least 3600 (silver Dirhams).

In his book, The Arab Civilization, the French historian, Gustave Le Bon described the Crusaders' entry into Jerusalem, saying:

> The Crusaders' behavior, when they entered Jerusalem, was quite different

from that of the tolerant Caliph Omar bin Al-Kattaab towards the Christians when he entered the city a few centuries earlier.[38]

In turn, the priest of Bolol City, Raymond Dagile, described this incident in history by saying:

What happened among the Arabs when our people [the Christians] conquered Jerusalem's walls and towers was really puzzling; some of them [the Muslims] were head-cut, others were stabbed, so that they were forced to throw themselves down the walls, others were burnt alive, so there could not be along Jerusalem roads except Arabs' heads, legs, and hands, so that we cannot avoid walking in corpses and this was just a sample of what happened.[39]

Khalil Toutah and Bolous Shehadeh (Christian writers) recounted that massacre, declaring that:

What the Crusaders did in the place where Jesus was crucified and buried (according to the Christian Bible) is really shameful and sinful. Jesus taught his disciples to love their enemies; but the crusaders, whose ideal was the holy cross, killed women, children and the elderly people. Even those who escaped to Aqsaa were followed by Godephry who was known as the protector of the Holy Tomb, and when he was in Java to fight the Egyptians, he

---

38 - Gustave le Bon **The Arab Civilization**. (tr. Adel Zueiter).
39 - **In** Al-Quds History and Views. **Pp.18 -19.**

became sick and asked his followers to take him back to Jerusalem where he died. He was buried in the Nativity Church.[40]

Unfortunately, the crusade is not a thing of the past, as some might think. It continued with many influential Christian influential personalities of the present. Though many Christians positively regard it, Jews and Muslims, on the other hand, maintain very bitter memories about its bloody history. Christian missionaries of the past and the present view their work of seducing people to convert as a crusade. Politicians view their double standard policy against other nations as a crusade. In other words, tolerating others is not part of the Christian agenda. It is not fair to deny the original teachings of the prophets (PBUT). They taught tolerance and practiced it. They brought guidance and light. However, the grave distortions of their teachings resulted in crusades, inquisitions, slavery, discrimination, colonization and treating people with double standards.

2. Christians and Jews in Palestine under Muslim rule

In contrast to the bleak history of the crusaders in Palestine, the Muslims have set a universal example for tolerance and accommodation that no nation on earth can claim its like. Abu Ubaydah, the Muslim Commander, sent to Omar bin al-Khattab (the second Muslim Caliph) telling him that the citizens of Jerusalem wanted him to come to take the keys of the city. Therefore, the caliph started his journey with his steward heading towards Jerusalem. On his arrival, the citizens of Elia (Jerusalem) received him with pleasure. He signed with them the famous peace document, which reads

---

40 - **Khalil Toutah and Bolous Shehadeh.** Jerusalem's History and Guide. **Jerusalem, 1480. P. 28.**

as follows:

> In the name of Allah, The Compassionate,
> The Merciful! This is what the Servant of
> God, Omar, Amir of the believers, gave to
> Elia's inhabitants concerning the safety of
> their properties, money, churches, etc.
> Their churches should not be demolished.
> They should not be harmed or forced to
> accept a religion against their will. This
> should be guaranteed by the Khalifah and
> all Muslims, and monitored by Allah and
> His Prophet (PBUH), as long as the other
> side adheres to it and pays the Jezyah.

As a matter of fact, Omar was the first to liberate Jerusalem from the Roman occupation.

3. Islam in Spain

During the 7th century, the people of Spain were given the choice to accept Islam willingly and peacefully as hundreds of thousands of people around the world are accepting Islam today. However, with the papal approval in 1479, Prince Ferdinand and Princess Isabella executed the unimaginably bloody history of the Spanish Inquisition, where notorious and indescribable persecutions and tortures against Muslims and Jews took place. The purpose was to force them to accept Christianity or be tortured to death. With the collapse of Granada, the last Muslim stronghold in Spain, into the hands of the Spaniards in 1492, Muslims were like an unprotected herd of cattle that were attacked by hungry wolves. So, they were massacred, enslaved and compelled to embrace Christianity at the edge of the sword.

In his article "When the Moors Ruled Spain", Thomas J. Abercrombie revealed many facts about the contributions with which Muslims had presented the West. He also alluded to the justice of the Islamic rule: where Jews, Christians and Muslims lived peacefully side by side for more than seven centuries. Then he shifted 180 degrees to talk in brief about atrocities committed by the Catholic Christians afterwards:

> It was here, long after Alfonso VI that the first victims of a growing Christian bigotry perished at the stake. In 1469 Prince Ferdinand of Aragon wed Princess Isabella of Castile. While waging war against the Moors to the south, they would view as a threat the Muslims and Jews in their own lands. In 1480, they established the Spanish Inquisition. Before it was over, three centuries later, thousands of Muslims and Jews had died; an estimated three million people were driven into exile. Short of its leading businessmen, artists, agriculturalists, and scientists, Spain would soon find itself a victim of its own cruelty.[41]

Irving (1973) in his book The Falcon of Spain, described the position of Christians and Jews under the tolerant Muslim rule as:

> Side by side with the new rulers lived the Christians and Jews in peace. The latter, rich with commerce and industry, were content to let the memory of oppression by the priest-ridden Goths sleep, [Jews had been virtually eliminated from the Spanish Peninsula in the seventh century by the

---

41 - **Thomas J. Abercrombie. When the Moors Ruled Spain.** National Geographic, **July 1988, P. 96.**

Christians.] now that the prime authors of it had disappeared. Learned in all the arts and sciences, cultured and tolerant, they were treated by the Moors [Muslims of Spain] with marked respect, and multiplied exceedingly all over Spain; and, like the Christian Spaniards under Moorish rule - who were called Mozarabes - had caused to thank their new masters for an era of prosperity such as they had never known before.[42]

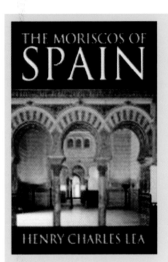

Such kind of tolerance had marked the relationship between Muslims and Christians and Jews. Muslims gave the Christians the chance to decide on their own. Gibbon (1823) stressed the fact that the Muslims of Spain abided by the teachings of Islam; they did not oppress the Christians and the Jews and Spain, but rather treated them with unparalleled tolerance.

> In times of tranquility and justice, the Christians have never been compelled to renounce the Gospel or to embrace the Qur'an.[43]

Lea, the great historian, in his book The Moriscos of

---

42 - **T. Irving.** The Falcon of Spain. **1973, p. 72.**
43 - **E. Gibbon.** The Decline and Fall of the Roman Empire VI, **1823, p. 453.**

Spain, pointed out that the papal brief, which Pope Clement VII in 1524 issued, was a bill freeing Charles V from all obligations resulting from the binding promises he had made to protect the life, religion, and the property of Muslims and Jews. It reads as follows:

> It recites the papal grief at learning that in Valencia, Catalonia and Argon, Charles has many subjects who are Moors (Muslims) and with whom the faithful cannot hold intercourse without danger; they even live with the temporal lords who make no effort for their conversion, all of which is a scandal to the faith and dishonor to the emperor, besides which they serve as spies, for those in Africa to whom they reveal the design of the Christians. It therefore exhorts Charles to order the inquisitors to preach the word of God to them and if they persist in their obstinacy the inquisitors shall designate a term and warn them that on its expiration they shall be exiled under pain of perpetual slavery, which shall be rigorously executed. The tithes of their temporal possessions, which they have never hitherto paid, shall accrue to their lords in recompense for the damage caused to them by the expulsion, under condition that the lords shall provide the churches with what is necessary for divine service, while the revenues of the mosques shall be converted into benefices. The portentous document concludes with a formal release to Charles

from the oath sworn to the Cortes not to expel the Moors; it absolved him from all censures and penalties of perjury thence arising and grants him whatever dispensation is necessary for the execution of the premises. Moreover, it confers on the inquisitors ample faculties to suppress all opposition with censures and other remedies, invoking if necessary the aid of the secular arm notwithstanding all apostolical constitutions and the privileges and statues of the land.[44]

This consent from the supreme Catholic authority unleashed the most indescribable form of savagery and intolerance against the Muslims of Spain at the hands of dreadful inquisitors.

The Muslims were given the choice of either accepting Christianity or death. When the village (Manices) surrendered, they were forcibly led to the church in batches of twenty to twenty five, and baptized, although they made it quite obvious that they were not consenting to their conversion.[45]

Those who resisted the barbaric compulsion faced a terrible fate.

They were all collected in a nearby castle and were 'massacred to man'[46]

It would be unfair to claim that all today's Christians would approve of this. Nonetheless, the highest Christian

---

44 - **H. C. Lea. 1901.** The Moriscos of Spain. **P.85.**
45 - Lea, p.63
46 - Lea, p.64

authority of that time led its full support to such utmost atrocities. The Christian authorities of today are hesitant to candidly renounce them, claim the responsibility, provide a public apology and stop all form of misinformation and distortions against Islam and Muslims.

4. Christianity During the Era of Colonization

Many church leaders had indicated that non- Christians do not have the right to live a good life and practice a faith of their own choice. Such premises have become non-negotiable principles in the minds of many. This very mentality is clearly spelled out through the suggestion made by the 'Bishop' of Winchester to Henry II of England:

> Let these dogs (Mongols and Muslims) destroy one another and be utterly exterminated and then we shall see the Universal Catholic Church founded on their ruins and there will be one fold and one shepherd.[47]

This was not only a singular attitude of this 13th century clergy, but rather that of some of the most prominent evangelists. Zwemer, who is looked to by Christian evangelists as having been almost a prophet, said:

> We must add to all this the utter collapse of Muslim political power in Africa, Europe and Asia. We, however, believe when the crescent wanes, the Cross will prove dominant, and that the disintegration of Islam is a divine preparation for the evangelization of Moslem lands....[48]

---

47 - **Stephen Neill.** A History of Christian Missions. **Penguin Books Ltd., New York, 1977, P. 118.**

48 - **Lyle L. Van der Werff.** Christian Missions to Muslims. **William Carey Library, California. 1977, P. 238.**

It might be argued by Christian apologists that such are the ideas of a person who is not really a part of the mainstream evangelists. But Zwemer is indeed considered as one of the most prominent figures in theorizing the Christianization of Muslims. In the Colorado 1978 conference, hundreds of delegates suggested the establishment of an institute named after Zwemer in Altadena, California, for the sole purpose of researching how to attack the Muslims in their belief.

While Muslims can invite people to the natural religion of Allah, The Supreme Being and the Creator of the universe and whatever therein, and believing in all the messengers of Allah including Jesus (peace and blessings of Allah be upon him), Christian missionaries execute all means to seduce and buy the hearts of the needy, sick and illiterate people under the cover of humanitarian aid while waging an unjust media campaign of misinformation and propaganda against Islamic teachings. Don M. Mc Curry[49] mentioned:

> Many times we were compelled to face the accusation that we use [my bold] any material, health and educational means to create [my bold] Christians among the Muslims who face very difficult and desperate situations.[50]

5. Islam in Europe:

To realize the standards and ethics that the Western World Order is built upon, one must ponder on Huntington's response in the Foreign Affairs regarding the Muslim's ac-

---

49 - A leading evangelist and the current director of Samuel Zwemer Institute.

50 - In Robert C. Petkept and R. L. Macacaba. *Food and Healthcare as Means for Muslim Evangelism.* The Gospel and Islam: A 1978 Compendium. **Don M.Mc Curry (ed.). P. 826.**

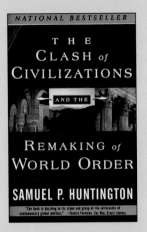

> **A world of clashing civilizations, however, is inevitably a world of double standards: people apply one standard to their kin-countries and a different standard to others.**
> -Samuel P. Huntington. *Clash of Civilizations.*

cusation of the Western World Order-as being biased and applying double standards,

A world of clashing civilizations, however, is inevitably a world of double standards: people apply one standard to their kin-countries and a different standard to others.[51]

Such double standards applied by the western world, the surrogate father of the New World Order, against the Muslims in Bosnia, Palestine, Chechnya, Azerbaijan and many other places all over the world are clear indicators of the western unjust treatment of other, non-Christian societies, including the Muslims.

As a matter of fact, it was the Vatican headed by the Pope who was determined to provide strong backing to the oppressing Catholic country in the Bosnia conflict, Croatia. Hence, according to Huntington, the Vatican extended recognition even before the European Community.[52]

---

51 - **Samuel Huntington. Clash of Civilizations. (**Foreign Affairs. **Summer, 1993, P.36).**

52 - Huntington. 1993. P.37.

Capricious actions against hundreds of thousands of oppressed people who went through vicious genocides and experienced unheard-of-atrocities of rape in the human history were carelessly dealt with by countries carrying the banners of the new world order.

Islam does not allow treating even one's enemies with injustice. Islam is innocent from any malpractices that may be committed by ignorant Muslims, even if they claim that they are doing them in the name of Islam.

I think it is one of the greatest tragedies and shame written with the blood of innocent people in the memory of history for generations of Muslims and peace loving people to remember. Especially, when compared with the Islamic system of justice and tolerance that does not allow treating even one's enemies with injustice. Islam is innocent from any malpractices that may be committed by ignorant Muslims, even if they claim that they are doing them in the name of Islam.

6. Islam in the Indian Subcontinent

Islam was firstly introduced into the Indian subcontinent during the 7th century and the Muslim dominance continued over India under the succeeding states until the British invasion in 1857, lasting for more than 1100 years. Had the Christian method of inquisition and conversion at the point of the gun been practiced, not a single Hindu would have been seen alive by the advent of the British colonialists to India. However, the Islamic tolerance and understanding of the nature of man manifested itself in India. In the Qur'an, Allah has clearly declared tolerance to be an essential ethical principle for mankind to follow.

Qutub Minar, Delhi, India

Islam came to India as well as to other parts of the world to transcend and elevate humanity above racism, ignorance, superstitions and injustice. Therefore, there was no need for forced conversion to the true religion of God. It is basically up to people to use the intellect with which God has bestowed upon them and make their choice. This is the reason as to why hundreds of thousands of people keep reverting to Islam as soon as they find out the truth about it. People embrace Islam by their own free will and without any seduction or compulsion. Many among them are scientists, politicians, lawyers, evangelists and even people of fame: Cat Stevens (now Yusuf Islam), the former famous pop singer; M. Hoffman, the German Ambassador to Morocco, who has recently written an eye-opening book titled, Islam is the Alternative; Morris Bucaille, the well known French scientist who accepted Islam after his long research in science and religion that is summarized in his book, The Bible, The Qur'an and Science; Mr. Olson, the current Danish Ambassador to Saudi Arabia who declared in a radio interview that :

If the people know the reality of Islam, millions will embrace it.[53]

The list of those who have sought the truth of Islam is too long to be mentioned here. It includes people from all walks of life.

7. Tolerance in Islam

When defining one of its important aspects, Islam means complete submission to Allah by choice and conviction, not through seduction or compulsion. Islam accommodates and welcomes all people as brothers and sisters regardless of their distinctive/particular affiliations or backgrounds. The Islamic attitude towards the followers of other religions is not only to show tolerance towards their beliefs, but also to affirm a non-negotiable Islamic principle of tolerance and religious responsibility.

There is no compulsion in [accepting} religion. The right course has become clear from error. So whoever disbelieves in taghut [i.e. false deities] and believes in Allah has grasped the trustworthy handhold with no break in it. And Allah is Hearing and Knowing. (The Qur'an 2: 256)

In fact, through the course of history of Islam, it has granted the people of other faiths the highest degree of tolerance by allowing them to follow their way, although some of their practices might have been in conflict with the religion of the majority. It was this degree of tolerance that the Muslims adopted towards their non-Muslim citizens.

There is another aspect of this matter which cannot be found in the written laws, nor can it be enforced by courts or the governments: this is the spirit of tolerance which un-

---

53 - The Islamic Magazine, **The Qur'an radio station 16/2/1415.**

derlies upright attitudes, benevolent dealings, respect for one's neighbors, and all the sincere sentiments of piety, compassion, and courtesy. Execution and report of such attitudes are required of every Muslim and cannot be obtained through constitutional legislation or court jurisdiction. The spirit of tolerance which can only be found in Islam is exclusively practiced in a true Islamic society.[54]

Many Qur'anic verses have emphasized dealings with non-Muslims with justice and respect, especially those who live in peace with the Muslims and do not raise enmity against them.

> Allah does not forbid you concerning those who do not fight you because of religion and do not expel you from your homes from being righteous towards them and acting justly towards them. Indeed, Allah loves those who act justly.
>
> (The Qur'an 60:8)
>
> And they give food in spite of their love for it to the poor, the orphan, and the captive, [Saying]: We feed you only for the acceptance of Allah. We wish neither from you reward nor gratitude.
>
> (The Qur'an 76: 8,9)

Although Muslims might disagree with other ideological systems and religious dogmas, it should not prevent them from demonstrating the correct manner of discussion and interaction with non-Muslims:

> And do not argue with the People of the Scripture except in a way that is best,

---

54- **Yusuf al-Qaradawi.** Non-Muslims in the Islamic Society. **(Tr. by K. M. Hamad and S.M. A. Shah) American Trust Publication, Indianapolis, 1985. P. 28.**

except for those who commit injustice
among them, and say we believe in that
which has been revealed to us and
revealed to you. And our God and your God
is One; and we are Muslims [in
submission] to Him.

(The Qur'an 29: 46)

In this context it seems appropriate to raise the question: Is tolerance of other religions as preached by Islam a
matter left to the Muslims to decide about? As a matter of
fact, tolerance in Islam has ideological basis in the Qur'an
and the teachings of Prophet Muhammad (pbuh), and it is
not subject to any human interference. Therefore, it is a constant Islamic principle that does not change over time or
place. According to the Qur'an, every human being is to be
honored as Allah has honored him/her:

And we have certainly honored the children
of Adam, and carried them on the land and
sea and provided for them of the good
things and preferred them over much of
what We have created with [definite]
preference.

(The Qur'an 17:70)

Islam is the final revelation of Allah the Almighty and
it is the religion of universal truth for all mankind. All of its
doctrines can withstand any challenge. Therefore, the existence of various religions--man-made or supposedly revealed religions--is only to allow the human intellect to
choose. The following verses of the Qur'an emphasize these
principles:

Allah witnesses that there is no deity except
Him, and [so do] the angels and those of
knowledge - [that He is] maintaining [creation]

In Islam, injustice is regarded as one of the greatest sins. Therefore, oppressing people because they have different beliefs is rejected. Prophet Muhammad (PBUH) said: The supplication of an oppressed person, even though he be a pagan, is heard (by Allah) directly, without any veil.

in justice. There is no deity except Him, the Exalted in Might, the Wise. Indeed, the religion in the sight of Allah is Islam. And those who were given the Scripture did not differ except after knowledge had come to them, out of jealous animosity between themselves and who ever disbelieves in the verses of Allah, then indeed, Allah is swift in [taking] account.[55]

(The Qur'an 3:18-19)

And had your Lord willed, those on earth would have believed, all of them entirely. Then will you compel the people until they become believers?

(The Qur'an 10: 99)

In Islam, injustice is regarded as one of the greatest

---

55 - In the actual world as it is, man has been endowed with various faculties and capacities, so that he should strive and explore and bring himself into harmony with Allah's will. Hence faith becomes a moral achievement, and to resist faith becomes a sin. As a complementary proposition, men of faith must not be angry if they have to contend against disbelief. And most important of all, they must guard against the temptation of forcing faith, i.e. imposing it on others by physical compulsion. Forced faith is no faith (Part of the translator's comment on the 10:99 verse, The Noble Qur'an, King Fahad Printing Complex, PP. 556,557).

sins. Therefore, oppressing people because they have different beliefs is rejected. Prophet Muhammad (PBUH) said:

> The supplication of an oppressed person, even though he be a pagan, is heard (by Allah) directly, without any veil.[56]

8. Concluding Remarks

To sum it up, intolerance has been a permanent practice of those in power represents Judaism, Christianity and Hinduism, and sometimes indoctrinated in their scriptures. They either shut off a segment of humanity or bring it in simply to persecute it. To be killed or converted was, at least until recently, the only choice confronting non-Christians in a Christian society or non-Hindus in a Hindu society. People of different religions have lived in prosperity and enjoyed the freedom to practice their faith. Some even sought asylum to escape religious persecution, as in the case of the Jews of Spain.

Misery of people in the form of poverty or illness is invested upon to change the belief of others. Stephen Neill has illustrated the scope of such inhumane monopoly of people suffering by saying:

> It was often a short period of the arrival of the missionary Lavigari to Algeria that cholera widespread. As a result of which a famine took place. He was able to collect 1800 orphan children after he had received permission from the French authorities to convert them to Christianity; then provide them with Christian education in some settlements that were labeled The

---

56 - **Related by Imam Ahmed in his** Musnad. **As reported in** al-Qaradwi 1985.

Christian Villegas. Such steps encouraged other missionaries in other countries to do just the same. They started by buying children as slaves, and then gathered them in Christian Settlements.[57]

Neil continues talking about such incidents supporting his arguments by statistics of buying the souls as well as the beliefs of needy people by saying:

This process (buying children and Christianizing them) has succeeded to the exact that some missionaries by the year 1902 were able to establish in one area, 250 farms containing 5000 salve children.[58]

Sigrid Hunke, the great German philosopher and historian, referred in her book *Allah ist ganz anders* to part of the letter that Oliverous, the theological philosopher who wrote a letter in 1221 to Saladdin (SalahuDeen) expressing his deep appreciation to the noble treatment the captured crusader soldiers received after their defeat in the battle of Hittin by writing:

For centuries, nobody has heard of such mercy and generosity, especially towards a brutal enemy's prisoners of war. When God decreed that we should fall at your hands, we did not see in you a ruthless tyrant. Instead, we new you as merciful father who showered us with his kindness and bounties as well as a supporter in hard times. And who would doubt that such generosity and tolerance was from Allah?...

57 - **Stephen Neill.** A History of Christian Missionaries. **Penguin Books, 1979, PP. 42 - 429.**
58 - Neil, 1979. P.429

The men that we have killed their parents, sons, daughters, brothers and sisters; and made them taste the most cruel torture, when we became their prisoners and we were about to die out of hunger, they treated us in the best way possible and preferred us over themselves. They did so while we were helpless and powerless.[59]

Hunke went on to report some of the most unimaginable atrocities that the crusaders have done against the Muslim civilians in Palestine. One of these incidents was when King Richard, The Lion's Heart, dishonored his reputation in the most demeaning way when he violated his oath to three thousand Muslim prisoners and ordered them to be slaughtered. The French king did the same.[60]

Provided to the reader below is a segment of an article which has been written by one of the prominent American thinkers, Professor John L. Esposito, in which he summarized the tolerance of Islam and Muslims during the peak of their power:

Christians and Jews were regarded as People of the Book (those who had possessed a Scripture (revelation from God). In exchange for allegiance to the state and payment of a poll tax, these protected (dhimmi) peoples could practice their faith and be governed by their religious leaders and law in matters of faith and

---

59 - **Sigrid Hunke,** Allah ist ganz anders. **SKd Bavaria Verlag & Handel Gmbh: Munchen, p. 25 (It was the author's translation from the Arabic version into English)**
60 - Hunke, p.25-6.

private life (family laws).[61]

Prince Charles was very candid in his speech about Islam and the West at the Oxford center for Islamic Studies when he said:

> Medieval Islam was a religion of remarkable tolerance for its time, allowing Jews and Christians the right to practice their inherited beliefs and setting an example which was not, unfortunately, copied for many centuries in the West...[62]

Thus, Islam has proven to be more tolerant than the imperial Christianity, providing greater religious freedom for Jews and Christians. Most local Christian Churches had been persecuted as schematics heretics by a foreign Christian Orthodoxy. Islam as a universal system tolerates peoples of different religious backgrounds and protects the rights of its diverse subjects against oppression and discrimination. At the same time, it emphasizes that it is the only absolute truth with ample objective and logical evidence. Tritton expressed his opinion regarding this very great attribute of tolerance in Islam by saying "The picture of the Muslim soldier advancing with a sword in one hand and the Qur'an in the other is quite false."[63]

Only Islam preaches and practices tolerance as part of its fundamental teachings that allows no second interpretation. Regardless of any deviation in part of the Muslims at

---

61 - **John L. Esposito. Islam and Christianity Fact to Face: An old conflict and prospects for a new ending.** Common well. **January 31st, 1997, P.12.**

62 - **Prince Charles, " Islam and the West."** Arab News, **October 27, 1993. In R. Hill Addulsalam.** Women's Ideal Liberation. **Abul-Qasim Publishing House: Jeddah, pp. 41-3.**

63 - A.S.Trittonin"Islam,"1951.inhttp://web.ionsys.com/~remedy/Islam%20and%20the%20Prophet%20God.htm

any time in history, which is seldom, the word of the Creator will always prevail. Through the many random examples of Islamic tolerance I selected from the writings of mostly non-Muslim writers, Islam has manifested an unparalleled form of tolerance. At a time when it asserts that it is the only system that contains the full truth as revealed and kept in tact in the real words of the Creator 'The Qur'an". This tolerance in the human sphere has allowed Islam to extend open-mindedness to the intellectual sphere, the topic of my next section.

●

CHAPTER III
Universality and Promotion of Science

This section of the book is devoted first to examining some of the systems of life adopted in our world nowadays. Following the examination we should be able to decide which system best accommodates our needs for development and better life styles. It should also help us determine those which hinder civilization and advancement, as well as those which give no priority to the values and ethics that underpin man's social, psychological and physical well-being. For a universal system to succeed, we need to adopt the one that is able to meet and balance our needs for a better life and prevent any transgression that may result in the destruction and extinction of mankind.

1. Buddhism, Hinduism, and Science

If we take Buddhism into consideration as a proposed universal way of life, it is easily realized that true Buddhism means complete devotion to idol worshipping and spending

one's time in complete seclusion and isolation from the surrounding world, which is full of injustice. Man, according to
Buddhism, is viewed as a source of evil. In order for him to
acquire righteousness, he must abandon this world and live
in complete isolation. Such a philosophy can never succeed
in bringing about peace of mind for its followers.

In both Hinduism and Buddhism, the world is regarded
as evil, and salvation is understood as its rejection, namely,
as freedom from the world. Moreover, these religions make
salvation a personal, individualistic affair, since they define it
in terms of states of consciousness, which can be only personal. Interaction with the outside world is viewed as evil.[64]

Whatever social order which has been developed by
the Hindus in terms of a state, an empire, a civilization or a
distinctive human community was done in deviation from
their teachings. Today's India based its system of government on democracy, regardless of the Hindu parties that
play a major role in Indian politics.

I think that such attitudes towards life cannot be accepted in a world like ours where great advances in technology have taken place and become an integral part of our
lives. No doubt, many of these advances in industry have
brought many unwanted side effects in both social and
health-related areas of society. A modern atheistic civilization, to the other extreme, gives man the full liberty to involve
himself in all aspects with no limits or respect to either nature or people. That can be seen in the irresponsible practices in genetic engineering and the destruction of ecology.
Purely material gains have blindfolded the eyes of the devel-
opers against the devastating moral, social and health problems that are posing unprecedented threats to humankind.

---

64 - Al- Faruqi, 1404, P. 101.

The need is urgent for a system that is not manipulated by the narrow materialist interests of a careless greedy minority; and at the same time striking a balance between man's needs for advancement in science and technology.

The materialistic solutions that seldom succeed are always sought. Aids, cancer, poverty, illiteracy, smoking, drugs, alcohol and many other social problems have grown at escalating rates. Materialistic gains have become major goals at the expense of values and morals. However, seceding at the other extreme of rejecting any involvement in the worldly affairs goes against the true nature of man. The need is urgent for a system that is not manipulated by the narrow materialist interests of a careless greedy minority; and at the same time striking a balance between man's needs for advancement in science and technology.

2. Islam and Science

Islam solves this dilemma by taking a moderate stance in relation to this issue. Man is not denied the right to enjoy life providing that he does not violate the rights of other creations of Allah as described by Him in the Qur'an- 7: 31-32

O Children of Adam! Wear your good clothing at every masjid, but be not excessive. Indeed, He [i.e., Allah] likes not those who commit excess. Say, Who has forbidden Allah's adornment, which He has produced for His servants and the lawful things of provision? Say, They are for those who believe during worldly life [but] exclusively for them on the Day of Resurrection. Thus do We explain in detail the verses for a people who know.

Any system of life that hinders advancement of humanity in sciences and technology that are of the benefit of humanity is not worthy of being chosen as a way of life. Islam stands tall in this regard, since it is the only religion that has opened the doors for great leaps in all fields of sciences. Muslims do not succeed in science and technology when they distance themselves from the pure teachings of Islam. Colonialists and orientalists discovered that fact, and hence tried to distract Muslims away from the real source of development. Many historians have recognized this fact. Among them, Philip Hitti, who says while referring to Al-Khawarzmi, a celebrated Muslim scholar in the field of mathematics:

One of the best scientific minds of Islam, Al-Khwarizmi, is undoubtedly the man who exercised the most influence on mathematical thought during the whole of the Middle Ages.[65]

M. Charles, a French scientist, refers to the contribution of another Muslim mathematician, Al-Battani, by saying:

65 - **Philip K. Hitti.** Precis deHistoire des Arabes. **(Short History of the Arabs). Payot, Paris,1950.**

Al-Battani was the first to use in his works the expressions sine and cosine. He introduced it to geometric calculus and calls it *extended shadow*. It is what is called in modern trigonometry the tangent.[66]

Historians stress that modern sciences are indebted to the Muslims for great advances in many of the scientific fields. As Fauriel (1846) states:

Contact between the two civilizations-- Christian and Muslim-- had been established by normal and well-founded routes. In this, commerce and pilgrimage played the principal role. Land and sea traffic between East and West was already flourishing well before the XIth century. It was through Spain, Sicily and the South of France, which were under direct Saracen rule that Islamic civilization entered into Europe.[67]

By the middle of the IXth century, Muslim civilization had already prevailed in Spain. The Spaniards of that time regarded Arabic as the only medium for science and literature. Its importance was such that the Ecclesiastical Authorities had been compelled to have the collection of canons used in Spanish churches translated into the Romance languages, (the predecessors of modern Spanish) for the two languages were in current use throughout the whole of Muslim Spain. Christian Spain recognized this superiority of the Muslims. In about 830, Alphonse the Great, King of the

---

66 - **M. Charles.** Apercu historique des methodes en geometrie. **(Historical Outline of Geometrical Methods). In Bammate.**
67 - **In Haidar Bammate.** Muslim Contribution to Civilization. **American Trust Publications, 1962. P. 16.**

Austrians, had sent for two Saracen Muslim scholars to act as tutors for his son and heir.

After conducting a rigorous comparative research of the Bible and the Qur'an to the major discoveries of modern science, the French renowned scientist and member of the French Scientific Academy noticed the absence of any contradictions between the contents of the Qur'an and these discoveries. Furthermore, he found that the Qur'an describes both phenomenal and unseen worlds in a completely accurate way:

> 'The Qur'an follows on from the two revelations that preceded it and is not only free from contradictions in its narrations, the signs of the various human manipulations to be found in the Gospels, but provides a quality all of its own for those who examine it objectively and in the light of science, i.e. its complete agreement with modern scientific data. What is more, statements are to be found in it that are connected with science: and yet it is unthinkable that a man of Muhammad's time could have been the author of them. Modern scientific knowledge therefore allows us to understand certain verses of the Qur'an, which, until now, it has been impossible to interpret.[68]

3. The Impact of Muslim Sciences on Europe

The scientific renown of the Muslims had spread far and wide, and attracted the intellectual elite of the Western World to Andalusia, Sicily and to the south of Italy. At the

68 - **Morris Bucaille**. The Bible, the Qur'an and Science. **4th edition, p.268.**

same time when the Muslim civilization was prospering during the Middle Ages, the Christian world was living in complete darkness. Philip Hitti remarked:

> No other people made as important a contribution to human progress as did the Arabs, if we take this term to mean all those whose mother tongue was Arabic and not merely those living in the Arabian Peninsula. For centuries, Arabic was the language of learning, culture and intellectual progress for the whole of the civilized world, with the exception of the Far East. From the ninth to the twelfth century, there were more philosophical, medical, historical, religious, astronomical and geographical works written in Arabic than in any human language.[69]

It was the Muslims' advances in science and diffusion of knowledge that ignited the beginning of our contemporary progress in science and technology. Al-Nadawi comments on this by writing:

> Meanwhile, owing to the Islamic and Muslim scientific influences, the volcano of knowledge had burst in Europe. Its thinkers and scientists had broken the intellectual slavery. They boldly refuted the ecclesiastical theories, which were based on preposterous evidence, and proclaimed their own investigations. The

---

69 - Philip K. Hitti. Pre,cis d Histoire des Arabes. (Short History of the Arabs). Payot, Paris, 1950.

papal authority[70] reacted ruthlessly. It established the inquisitions to discover, and bring to book, the heretics lurking in towns, houses, cellars, caves and fields This institution performed its duty with such savage alacrity that a Christian theologian exclaimed that it was hardly possible for a man to be a Christian, and die in his   bed. It is estimated that between 1481 and 1801 the Inquisition punished three hundred and forty thousand persons, nearly thirty-two thousands of whom were burnt alive, including the great scientist, Bruno, whose only crime was that he taught the plurality of the worlds. Bruno was delivered to the secular authorities to be punished as mercifully as possible, and without the shedding of blood, which, in fact was the horrible formula for burning a prisoner at stake. Galileo, another scientist of no less worth, contrary to the scriptures, was tortured by the Inquisitions for maintaining that the earth moved around the sun.[71]

According to Draper in his book History of Conflict between Religion and Science, intellectual stagnation of the clergy and the atrocities perpetrated by the Inquisition led the enlightened sectors of the European society to revolt not only against the clergy and the church, but also against all the values and any type of truth that was not corrupted by

---

70 - How can the things and writings of those clergymen be accepted as the basis of today's Christianity?
71 - Al-Nadawi, P. 127.

the devious clergy.[72]

4. The Shallowness of Modern Science

The study of science, which Islam gave to the West, was to a large extent perfectly in accord with Allah's teachings. However, from the 14th century until today, Western societies have diverged from this Islamic scientific tradition. Islam requires that people take over the responsibility of developing science that benefits all people with no harm to others; while respecting nature. Islam also emphasizes a very important principle that science cannot be turned into god, because of a very simple reason, which is that, our knowledge is relative and conjectural, and therefore our sciences are also relative and conjunctural. Muhamed Qutb writes:

> The god of science has, however, turned out to be extremely fickle, ever changing and constantly shifting positions, upholding one thing as a fact and reality today and rejecting it the other day as false and spurious. Consequently its worshippers are doomed to a perpetual state of restlessness and anxiety, for how can they find rest and peace of mind under such a capricious god? That the modern West is afflicted with this uncertainty and restlessness is born out by the large number of psychological and nervous disorders that are so common in modern societies today.

He also adds:

---

72 - **Detailed information about this topic is found in J. W. Draper.** History of the Conflict between Religion and Science. **London, 1927.**

Yet another result of this defection of modern science is that the world we live in has become devoid of all meaning and purpose, with no higher order or power to guide it. Tension and conflict between different forces have become the order of the day. As a result everything in this world is changing.[73]

This misuse of science has affected all spheres of life--the political, economical, educational, healthy, even the presumably scientific world of facts. All these factors urge man to look for a system in which he may find satisfaction, peace, tranquility, and freedom from contradictions.

An example of such misguided science is the prejudice against blacks for a larger part of the USA. The rise of pseudoscientific racism and the popularity of social-engineering ideas among Latin American white elites militated against the social acceptance of the black population. The positivist followers of the French philosopher Auguste Comte thought Africans were far from ready for the stage of technical modernity, and neglected them. Adherents of social Darwinism considered the African dimension of the pluralistic society a sign of fundamental weakness because they assumed the natural superiority of the white race.[74]

5. Why does Islam Encourage Science and Advancement?

Why is it so that Islam is the only system of life that

73 - Muhammad Qutb. *Islam and the Crisis of the Modern **World***. Islam its Meaning and Message. **Khushid** Ahmed. The Islamic Foundation, London. 1980. P. 244.
74 - Black in the Americas, Microsoft (R) Encarta (R) 96 Encyclopedia. (c) 1993-95 Microsoft Corporation. All rights reserved. (c) Funk & Wagnall Corporation. All rights reserved.

Why is Islam the only religion that can meet the needs of humanity and integrate and interact with the universe in a harmonious way? It is simply because all other religions and dogmas have never adopted a true monotheistic way of life. They emphasized the personification of god through nature. They also assumed that contradiction was a principle characteristic of knowledge.

can integrate man's needs for advancement and discovery of the universe around him? The features that distinguish Islam from other beliefs led Gibb (a well-known orientalist) to write:

> The kind of society that a community builds for itself depends fundamentally upon its belief as to the nature and purpose of the universe and the place of the human soul within it. This is a familiar enough doctrine and is reiterated from Christian pulpits week after week. But Islam possibly is the ONLY religion, which has constantly aimed to build up a society on this principle. The prime instrument was law (Shreia'h).[75]

Why is Islam the only religion that can meet the needs

---

75 - **H.A.R. Gibb.** Modern Trends in Islam, **pp. 86-7.**

of humanity and integrate and interact with the universe in a harmonious way? It is simply because all other religions and dogmas have never adopted a true monotheistic way of life. They emphasized the personification of god through nature. They also assumed that contradiction was a principle characteristic of knowledge. Therefore, during a period of more than 1000 years, when Christianity, for example, took control of peoples' minds, this era did not produce any natural sciences. Christians, Hindus, Buddhists, etc. could not adopt a scientific attitude until Islam liberated them from their polytheism[76], which was imposed by religious authorities, and until they were exposed to the Muslim scientific revolution. Neither Hinduism, Buddhism nor Christianity could elevate their followers to engage in scientific thinking. Nevertheless, as soon as they became Muslims and worshipped the Almighty God alone, they became scientists and great thinkers side by side with the Muslim Arabs of that era. Examples from history as presented above are great witnesses.

Muslims were able to acquire the qualities needed for scientific thinking and advancement for two main reasons: firstly, the Glorious Qur'an and the Noble traditions of Prophet Muhammad urged the people to contemplate and study their own nature as well as themselves and the universe around them.

Indeed, Allah is Exalted in Might and Forgiving.

(The Qur'an 35:28)

---

76 - **Examples of this are Trinity in Christianity, and worship of Saints and the great influence of priests. As for Hinduism, Gustave le Bon mentioned in his classic book** Les Civilization de l Inde **that The Vedas give the number of Hindu gods as 33. During this period, as many as 33 million gods were worshipped by Hindus. Almost everything that possessed any attractiveness or utility had been   vested with divine attributes. pp. 440-1.**

Say, Are those who know equal to those
who do not know? Only they will remember
[who are] people of understanding.

(The Qur'an 39:9)

Allah will raise those who have believed
among you and those who were given
knowledge by degrees. And Allah is
acquainted with what you do.

(The Qur'an 58:11)

Then, do they not reflect upon the Qur'an?
If it had been from [any] other than Allah,
they would have found within it much
contradiction.

(The Qur'an 4:82)

Do those who disbelieve not see that the
heavens and earth were a joined entity,
then We separated them, and made from
water every living thing? Then will they not
believe?

(The Qur'an 21:30)

We will show them Our Signs in the
horizons and within themselves until it
becomes clear to them that it is the truth.
But is it not sufficient concerning your Lord
that He is over all things a Witness?

(The Qur'an 41: 53)

Many of these signs have been thoroughly discussed
in the Qur'an and later on discovered by scientists as they
progress in their knowledge and their scientific techniques
in research development. The following excerpt refers to a
single sign that scientist found great details in the Qur'an.

Or (the unbelievers' state) is like the
darkness in a deep sea. It is covered by

waves, above which are waves, above which are clouds. Darknesses, one above another. If a man stretches out his hand, he cannot see it....

(Qu'ran, 24:40)

This verse mentions the darkness found in deep seas and oceans, where if a man stretches out his hand, he cannot see it. The darkness in deep seas and oceans is found around a depth of 200 meters and below. At this depth, there is almost no light (see the figure below). Below a depth of 1000 meters there is no light at all. Human beings are not able to dive more than forty meters without the aid of submarines or special equipment. Human beings cannot survive unaided in the deep dark part of the oceans, such as at a depth of 200 meters and deeper.

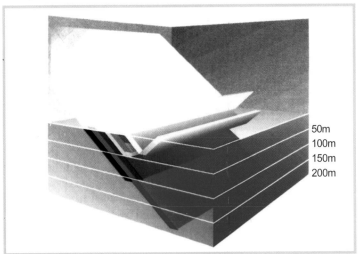

Figure: Between 3 and 30 percent of the sunlight is reflected at the sea surface. Then almost all of the seven colors of the light spectrum are absorbed one after another in the first 200 meters, except the blue light. (Oceans, Elder and Pernetta, p. 27.)

Scientists have recently discovered this darkness by means of special equipment and submarines that have enabled them to dive into the depths of oceans

We can also understand from the following sentences in the previous verse, "...in a deep sea. It is covered by waves, above which are waves, above which are clouds....", that the deep waters of seas and oceans are covered by waves, and above these waves are other waves. It is clear that the second set of waves is the surface waves that we see, because the verse mentions that above the second waves there are clouds. But, what about the first waves? Scientists have recently discovered that there are internal waves, which "occur on density interfaces between layers of different densities." (See the figure below).

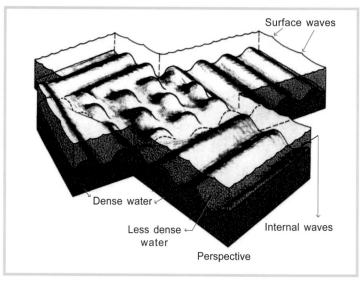

Internal waves at interface between two layers of water of different densities. One is dense (the lower one), the other one is less dense (the upper one). (Oceanography, Gross, p. 204.

The internal waves cover the deep waters of seas and oceans because the deep waters have a higher density than the waters above them. Internal waves act like surface waves. They can also break, just like surface waves. The human eye cannot see internal waves, but they can be detected by studying temperature or salinity changes at a given location.[77]

As a matter of fact, this verse that talks about how the universe was created has the very information by which two physicists were awarded the 1973 Nobel Prize. However, these scientific facts had already been revealed to Prophet Mohammed more than 1400 years ago.[78]

Secondly, Tawheed (the worship of Allah alone) is the essence on which Islam is built. It rejects all types of myths and superstitions, since they are the greatest enemies of science. Tawheed refers all aspects of causality to Allah. Therefore, scholars should be able to investigate and discover these relationships, know them, and then put them to the use of humanity.[79]

After the long and bitter struggle between science and other religions, Islam came to bring harmony between the religion of Allah and science in this century of science. In

77 - The above large excerpt was taken in its entirety from I. A. Ibraheem. A Brief Illustrated Guide to Understanding Islam. Darusalam: Houston, 2002, pp.20-22

78 - **Gary Miller. The Amazing Qur'an. Abul-Qasim Publishing House. PP. 33-34. For more information about the recently discovered scientific miracles of the Qur'an, see Maurice Bucailles' book,** The Bible, The Qur'an and Science. **Kazi Publications: Lahore, Keith Moore,** The Developing Human. **W.B. Saunders Company: Philadelphia, 1982.**

79 - **A very valuable book on this topic, entitled** Tawheed and its Influence on Thought and Life**, was written by Dr. Isma'il al-Farouqi, the late Chairman of the Department of Religious Studies at Temple University.**

this regard, the Muslim World League has established a commission that is specialized in investigating the scientifically proven facts as described in the Qur'an and Sunnah (teachings of Prophet Mohammad (pbuh).[80]

In summary, other ways of life (Christianity, Buddhism, Capitalism, Communism and Hinduism) have never come to a unified understanding of Allah, man or nature. Thus, their views of science have been fallacious. The unity of Islam allows a proper scientific perspective, which promotes advancement and development in the fields of science and technology. Such understanding of reality and the relation between the human being and nature in addition to the role Muslims should play in science is clearly illustrated in this quote from Dr. Mahathir Mohammed's speech at the Oxford Islamic Forum:

> In this modern world Muslims have a real mission. They must bring back the spiritual values to a world that is fast becoming Godless and thoroughly materialistic, so arrogant that it thinks it knows all the answers to everything; a world which will develop the ultimate means of destruction and place it on the hands of irresponsible and insane individuals; a world tittering in the brink of a man-made Apocalypse.

Presently, people want to create a world according to their wishes. They forget that for all their brilliance, they can hardly answer the "why" questions. They cannot answer why it works the way it does, why the universe operates in the way it does, why matter acts in the way it does, why oxygen

---

80 - The address of this commission is Commission on Scientific Miracles of Qur'an and Sunnah, Muslim World League, Makkah, Saudi Arabia.

and hydrogen form water,etc. Our scientific endeavor may provide different mechanisms to achieve adequate observation of and descriptive laws of the universe. Adequate explanatory ability will remain most of the time beyond the reach of purely human science. If any answers would emerge, they would only be conjectural.

The 21st Century is insignificant to the Muslims and non-Muslims alike. It is just a period in time, which will see many changes to which Muslims will be part of, regardless of their stand towards them. It is better if they faced it with their eyes wide open and with a clear vision of what they want to do and the role they wish to play. And if they chose to play a constructive role while retaining their faith, the spiritual values and brotherhood, they would be able to contribute positively to the development of humankind.[81]

I think it is appropriate to conclude this chapter with the words of the great historian of sciences, V. Robinson, in describing the situation of Muslim Spain during the Dark Ages in Europe. It is a reminder regarding the function of Islam as a genuine drive for guiding and benefiting science which its aim should be for the benefit of humanity:

> Europe darkened at sunset, Cordova shone with public lamps; Europe was dirty, Cordova built a thousand baths; Europe was covered with vermin, Cordova changed its garments daily; Europe lay in mud, Cordova's streets were paved; Europe's palaces had smoke-holes in the ceiling, Cordova's arabesques were exquisite; Europe's nobility could not sign

---

81 - **Mahathir Mohamad (The Malaysian Prime Minister) Muslims can be Positive Force in the 21st Century.** Islamic Future - **Vol. XIII-No. 71**

its name, Cordova's children went to
school; Europe's monks could not read
the baptismal service, Cordova's teachers
created a library of Alexandrian
dimensions.[82]

This conclusion leads to the fourth principle towards
which the universality of Islam points -- that it provides the
best solutions to the problems facing humankind rather than
creating new ones.   ●

---

82 - **V. Robinson,** The Story of Medicine, **p. 164, in Thomson 1996, For
Christ's Sake. Ta-Ha Publications: London, P.XI**

humanity today faces numerous critical problems, from individual problems such as, alcoholism and sexual diseases, to social problems such as, the dire conditions of the elderly, abuse of children and women, and pervasive global problems like wars of aggression.

CHAPTER IV

Universality and Solving Problems of Humanity

Humanity today faces numerous critical problems, from individual problems such as, alcoholism and sexual diseases, to social problems such as, the dire conditions of the elderly, abuse of children and women, and pervasive global problems like wars of aggression. If any system of life is proposed for humankind, it should be able to provide preventative measures for such problems. It should also be able to solve emerging problems. There is no doubt that the existence of the majority of our problems in the world is the result of the inability of the existing systems to neither prevent nor solve such problems. Indeed these systems often seem to encourage the manifestation of and root cause for these problems.

1. Alcoholism and Drug Addiction

Although some of the existing systems, especially the secular ones, have achieved considerable scientific and material success, which have brought positive changes and comfort to some, their negative impact and pressures have led for many people to resort to self-destructive actions and habits. Consumption of narcotics, drugs and alcohol has become a universal problem. The magnitude of these problems has transcended health and social consequences resulting in war between drug smugglers and countries where drug trafficking takes place on the one hand and countries of drug consumption on the other. The crimes of drug and alcohol users vary from public drunkenness or driving while intoxicated to committing rape, manslaughter and homicide.

In the year 1979 alone, police in the U.S. reported 2,137,999 alcohol-related crimes.[83] In fact, the dire effects of alcohol went far beyond this figure. In 1975, there were about 50,000,000 moderate drinkers and 14,000,000 heavy drinkers in the United States alone.[84] The reliance of many Americans on alcohol and drugs seems to have grown substantially and has emerged as one of the most costly social problems and the most difficult to control. One might be asked why has the problem of alcoholism become more serious in recent years? The answer of five leading American sociologists is:

The last decades in America were referred
to as the chemical age, in which people

---

83 - **Federal Bureau of Investigation,** Uniform Crime Reports, **1979 Washington, D.C.: U.S. Government Printing Office, 1980), PP. 196-197.**
84 - **Carl D. Chambers, James A. Inciardi, Harvey A. Siegal.** Chemical Coping : A Report on Legal Drug Use in the United States. **Spectrum Publications, Inc., New York, 1975.**

utilize a myriad of substances in order to cope with whatever problems they face: physical pain, emotional upset, or blocked aspirations. Some have gone so far as to argue that America is a drug culture, and when we consider the enormous quantity and variety of drugs consumed   by Americans each year, there may be some credence to this description.[85]

Realizing the magnitude of alcoholism and drug addiction, many countries have taken different measures. The United States, for example, banned the consumption and the selling of all forms of alcoholic beverages and other types of drugs in 1920. This was known as the Prohibition law, which lasted from 1920 to 1933. However, despite the might of the FBI and other law enforcement agencies, it resulted in great failure and perhaps could have never succeeded. As a matter of fact, the enactment of the National Prohibition Act was followed by widespread disregard of it. Illegal manufacturing, transportation and sale of alcoholic beverages became common. It provided organized criminals a very valuable source of business. The whole experiment resulted in a dismal failure.[86]

This very fatal problem is not peculiar to the US. Indeed, most societies of the world suffer greatly from alcoholism, more than any other drug. According to a report published in the year 2000 by the Russian daily news paper Kommersant,[87] two thirds of Russian men die drunk and

---

85 - Sullivan, Thompson, Wright, Gross and Spady (1980), P. 612.
86 - **Henry W. Mannle and J. David Hirschel.** Fundamentals of Criminology. **Delmar Publishing Inc. Albany, New York, 1982. P. 322.**
87 - Kommersant, Moscow, May 19, 2000, in Ben Adam (2006) "Alcohol: The Devil's Deadly Disease". http://www.islamreligion.com/articles/454/

According to a report published in the year 2000 by the Russian daily news paper Kommersant, two thirds of Russian men die drunk and more than half of that number dies in extreme stages of alcoholic intoxication.

more than half of that number dies in extreme stages of alcoholic intoxication. At 57.4 years, Russian men have the lowest life expectancy rate in Europe. The paper reported the results of a three year study of men aged between 20 and 55 in the cities of Moscow and Udmurita that:

> "Everyone is drunk: Murderers and their victims, drowning victims, suicides, drivers and pedestrians killed in traffic accidents, victims of heart attacks and ulcers."

Mr. Chernyenko, vice chairman of the National Organization of Russian Muslims, remarks on the matter of alcoholism:

> "One can say that drinking vodka or wine is a significant aspect of Russian culture, yet I can be a good Russian while not drinking alcohol... Most of the social problems in Russia are caused by alcohol consumption. If we can introduce some Islamic social values to Russia, the

society and the country will become stronger."

It is beyond doubt that neither Judaism nor Christianity or any other system can provide a workable solution to such a problem, because alcohol consumption is an essential part of most if not all their religious and official occasions even though it is prohibited according to the teachings of The Bible, the source of their teachings. As for drugs, it is evident that influential sectors of some nominally Christian governments do support the legalization of drugs or have initiated programs--such as the free distribution of syringes to addicts - which encourage drug addiction rather than containing it. During the last five years alone, the United States government has spent $52 billion in fighting drugs with little if any success.[88]

General Norman Schwarzkopf, Commander of the Allied Forces in the Gulf War addressed the US Congress on how the prohibition of alcohol consumption in Saudi Arabia made for better and more disciplined American soldiers, June 13, 1991):

> "Our sick call rate went down, our accident and injury rate went down, our incidents of indiscipline went down, and health of the forces went up. So there were some very therapeutic outcomes from the fact that no alcohol was available whatsoever in the Kingdom of Saudi Arabia."[89]

The Islamic Solution

Alcoholism and drug addiction have proven to be un-

88 - Family, **Vol. 14. 14 August, 1994. P. 9.**
89 - Gen. Norman Schwarzkopf address to the US Congress, June 13, 1991, in Ben Adam (2006) "Alcohol: The Devil's Deadly Disease". http://www.islamreligion.com/articles/454/

solvable problems to many sociologists and social activists, not to mention the police force and politicians. Unable
to stem their use, the societies where alcoholism and drug
abuse have become chronic have ceased addressing un-
derlying root causes. Instead, they concentrate on control-
ling the effects in a selective and piecemeal approach. For
instance, there is not a law that prevents the manufacture,
sale and the consumption of alcoholic beverages, though
there is one for driving while intoxicated. The effect, not the
root cause, is addressed here: the symptom, not the disease. Pilots can drink any time they want but not when handling airplanes. Liquor advertising is so prevalent that it has
indoctrinated children. Children cannot wait to reach eighteen years of age, so that they can hastily rush to the closest liquor store to buy alcohol by themselves for the first
time, as if it were a treat or 'the thing' to do.

All these contradictions and double standards are rejected in Islam. If alcohol is harmful while driving, then it should
be harmful at all times. If it is harmful for young people under
the age of eighteen, then it should be harmful for the people
at any age. The evidence to the contrary is the horrific number of crimes that are being committed under the influence
of alcohol or drugs.

Islam, the divine teaching of God, came to eliminate
this problem altogether; therefore, it leaves no opportunity
for its grave consequences to destroy human beings and
their societies. All avenues that lead to alcohol consumption
are legally blocked. So, instead of exploiting resources to
deal with the symptomatic aspects, the whole disease is
prevented. Islam aims, from the beginning, at raising the
consciousness of its followers. Thus, outside enforcement
is not necessary. One finds many places in the Qur'an where
Allah says:

Islam has established a whole system of life so that all its components work in harmony. Solutions that have been proposed all over the world to solve the problems in question are not compatible with other systems of the same society. As a result, they have led to social chaos.

O you who believe be aware of Allah

O you who have believed, be upright [in responsibility] for Allah, witnesses in justice, and do not let the hatred of a people prevent you from being just. Be just; that is nearer to righteousness. And fear Allah. Indeed, Allah is acquainted with what you do.

(The Qur'an 5:8)

Islam has established a whole system of life so that all its components work in harmony. Solutions that have been proposed all over the world to solve the problems in question are not compatible with other systems of the same society. As a result, they have led to social chaos. Fasting, one of the five pillars of Islam, for example, is an institution in Islam that encourages self-consciousness and self-disci-pline on the part of the followers.

Muslims are taught that Allah has made all good com-modities permissible and all the bad commodities prohib-ited, describing the believers as:

> Those who follow the Messenger, the unlettered prophet whom they find mentioned in what they have of the Torah and the Gospel [who] enjoins upon them what is right and forbids them from what is wrong and makes lawful for them the good things and prohibits them from the evil, and relieves them of their burden and the shackles which were upon them.
> (The Qur'an 7:157)

When such a belief is established in the hearts of the believers that the Creator of the universe has ordered people not to engage in certain actions or consume certain things, then the law is accepted. Such compliance by Muslims is typical of the early days of Islam. Quraishies (Makkahans) and other existing pre-Islamic peoples used to engage in drinking alcohol as a common social behavior just like the current non-Muslim societies. However, after submitting themselves to the will of Allah the Almighty, they stopped worshipping idols and drinking alcohol as soon as the call from Allah came, enjoining them:

> O you who have believed, indeed, intoxicants, gambling [sacrificing on] stone atters [to other than Allah] and diving arrows are but defilement from the handiwork of Satan, so avoid it, that you may be successful. Satan only wants to

cause between you enmity and hatred through intoxicants and gambling, and to obstruct you from the remembrance of Allah and from prayer. So will you not resist? And obey Allah and obey the Messenger and beware. And if you turn away, then know that upon Our Messenger is only [the responsibility for] clear notification.

(The Qur'an 5: 90-92)

People all over Madinah stopped drinking immediately. They instantly got rid of their reserves of alcohol to the extent that the roads of Madinah turned into streams of wine. They did not hesitate to respond immediately to the divine command. There was no need for the interference of highly trained agents or the exploitation of billions of dollars to stop this destructive habit. This is really where the strength of the Islamic system lies. The people themselves take the initiative and willingly submit, so that no course of action needs to be imposed on them. The welling submission to Allah is behind the decision of millions of people to accept Islam as a way of life:

There is no compulsion in [accepting} religion. The right course has become clear from error. So whoever disbelieves in taghut [i.e. false deities] and believes in Allah has grasped the trustworthiest handhold with no break in it. And Allah is Hearing and Knowing.

(The Qur'an 2: 256)

The willing submission in Islam should be contrasted with the grudging social submission of secularist societies. When the Law of Prohibition was imposed by the United

States government in the 1920's, people were not prepared spiritually or psychologically to abide by it. In effect, there was not a system of life in which such laws could be integrated. The force of a man-made law cannot go unchallenged when imposed on people who disagree with it. When there is not a common denominator, things fall apart, because the people live in Jahiliyah[90] (devastating ignorance).

2. Crime

Crime in its different forms - organized crime, street crimes, state crimes, social crimes, etc. - is considered a major threat to peace and security in our world. However, discussing in detail the magnitude of the problem of crime as a universal catastrophe is beyond the scope of this study. **A summary of statistics that describe the spread of some crimes in the U.S., based on U.S. Government references, is presented below:**

Year	Crime Index	Violent Crime	Property Crime	Murder	Rape
1976	11,349,700	1,004,210	10,345,500	18,780	57,080
1994	13,989,500	1,857,670	12,131,900	23,330	102,220
1976-95*	+5.0	+20.8	+2.9	+4.8	+6.6

Percentage of the increase in selected crimes between 1976 and 1995.[91]

90 - It refers to the period in history before Islam.
91 - These statistics are based on the FBI, Uniform Crime Report, 1995 as presented by The World Almanac and Book of Facts 1997.

The Uniform Crime Report (UCR) issued by the U.S. Federal Bureau of Investigation (FBI) revealed that the number of reported crimes in the U.S. (as in the table above) increased by 5.0 % in the years from 1976 to 1995. Arrests in 1985 totaled 11.9 million, an increase of 3% over 1984.[92] Though the numbers presented are extremely high for the most prosperous nation that presumably has one of the most advanced security systems, the UCR figures are widely believed by criminologists to be low. A more reliable index is probably the U. S. Bureau of Justice Statistics' National Crime Survey (NCS), an annual report on household crime victimization based on census surveyors. This survey covers crimes not reported to police. Its 1985 survey showed that 25% (1 in every 4 households in the U. S.) had experienced crimes against individual members of the household or against the household itself during that year.[93]

Regardless of the costly efforts by the FBI and the high loss of lives among police officers[94] to reduce crime rates in the United States, the reversal is occurring. According to FBI, Uniform Crime Reports (1995), the number of total reported offenses including murder, property crimes, rape, robbery, etc. has increased from 11,349,700 crimes in 1976 to 14,872,900 in 1992, an increase of 3,537,200 reported offenses.[95] And according to the most recent statistics from the Justice Department's Bureau of Justice Statistics, at the end of 2006, roughly in 1 in ever 31 adults in the

---

92 - The New Grolier Electronic Encyclopedia, 1991 edition, P. 19.
93 - Ibid, P. 20.
94 - According to the U.S. Federal Bureau of Investigation, during the years (1988- 96) 1187 police officers were killed and 1040799 were assaulted by firearms or other dangerous weapons.
95- **The World Almanac and Book of Facts 1997 in** Microsoft Bookshelf 98.

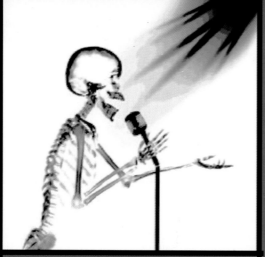

According to FBI, Uniform Crime Reports (1995), the number of total reported offenses including murder, property crimes, rape, robbery, etc. has increased from 11,349,700 crimes in 1976 to 14,872,900 in 1992, an increase of 3,537,200 reported offenses. After all these facts, can any sensible human being claim that the prime superpower and the leader of the New World Order that has gravely failed to reduce crime in its cities will succeed in restoring peace and security to the remainder of the world?

United States was in prison or jail, or on parole or in supervised release.[96] After all these facts, can any sensible human being claim that the prime superpower and the leader of the New World Order that has gravely failed to reduce crime in its cities will succeed in restoring peace and security to the remainder of the world?

As these statistics show, crime,[97] in its various forms, has become a major threat to societal and individual security. Crime from a Western perspective has been defined as: an act by a member of a given social group, which by the rest of the members of that group regard as so injurious

---

96 - http://www.realtruth.org/articles/071228-004-cm-print.html
97 - The Challenge of Crime in a Free Society (Washington, D.C.: U.S. Government Printing Office, 1967), P. 33.

or as showing such a degree of antisocial attitude in the perpetrator that the group publicly, overtly and collectively reacts by trying to abrogate (abolish) some of his rights- cited from the President's Commission on Law Enforce- ment and the Administration of Justice. Nevertheless, most of the methods used to fight against crime have backfired and are far short of meeting such a challenge. According to some recent statistics from the Bureau of Justice, during the late 1970's there were about 268,000 prison inmates in all 50 states. By the end of 2006, there were over 2.4 million. Despite this drastic increase, crime rates remained high.[98] Most of the statistical data collected are about Western so- cieties, due to the availability of documentation on the mat- ter. The failure of the Western methods of combating crime- -as attested by the continual rise of crime rates--leads one to suggest a solution which treats criminal activity not piece- meal but within the total scheme of life: a system that had restored peace and security to the lives of people from all nations that were under its folds.

The Islamic Solution

The Islamic concept of security is a very comprehen- sive one, more comprehensive than any of the other exist- ing systems. It looks at humankind in relation to the universe and its mass-influencing factors. It encompasses physical, mental, psychological, and spiritual domains as integral parts of an overall societal security system. Islamic teach- ings do not merely provide solutions to what is considered to be exceptional behavior in the form of crime, but emphati- cally focus on measures that prevent its occurrence. In other words, Islam provides as many means as possible to avert temptation. While modern societies flaunt temptation (liquor,

98 - http://www.realtruth.org/articles/071228-004-cm-print.html

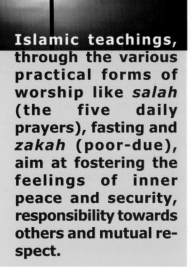

Islamic teachings, through the various practical forms of worship like *salah* (the five daily prayers), fasting and *zakah* (poor-due), aim at fostering the feelings of inner peace and security, responsibility towards others and mutual respect.

pornography, violence, etc.) before the people, a true Islamic society removes the sources of these temptations, and when the need for correction emerges, the punishment is serious and effective.

In most modern societies, crime has prospered because a completely contradictory approach is followed. All forms of temptation are prevalent. When it comes to correction, it is done leniently and frivolously. It is often biased and protective of the criminal's rights over those of the victim.

Islamic teachings, through the various practical forms of worship like salah (the five daily prayers), fasting and zakah (poor-due), aim at fostering the feelings of inner peace and security, responsibility towards others and mutual respect. In addition to their spiritual and moral functions they work as prevention against committing all evil behaviors. In a video film by the Christian Science Monitor about Islam in America, a large portion was devoted to describing the lives of maximum-security prison inmates before and after becoming Muslims. Before reverting to Islam, many were serial killers, drug smugglers and addicts, and professional criminals. When they embraced Islam while in prison, they turned into dignified, secure and contributing citizens. Western statistical indexes show that in the majority of maximum-security prisons, the criminals get involved in criminal acts and end up back in prison. Based on the Bureau of Justice (BJS), of all prisoners released in 1994 (the most recent nationwide study by the BJS), 67.5% were arrested with in three years.[99] As a matter of fact, in a recent article titled "Would God use prison to rehabilitate criminal minds?, the author emphasized that 'the problems inherent with this system have remained the same for years: recidivism (repeated relapse in criminal acts), overcrowding, cost and, most tellingly-despite the large amount of funding-the utter inability to reduce crime. Such statistics are reversed when those inmates become Muslims, according to Christian Science Monitor.[100] The success of Islam in providing the best solution to crimes in the midst of the American society where all types of correction programs have failed is strong prevalent evidence for the universality of Islam and the pressing need for the adoption of its teachings.

3. Abuse of Children and Women

People tend to think of the family as a social institution in which love and affection prosper. An establishment whose stockholders exchange support and care, in reality, the family in most modern world societies has become completely the opposite of what it is assumed to be. The problem is more pervasive in most modern societies allover the world.[101] According to American official statistics of crime, 20 percent of

---

99 - http://www.realtruth.org/articles/071228-004-cm-print.html
100 - Islam In America **(video). The Christian Science Monitor Publishing Society, Boston, Mass. 1992.**
101 - According to the FBI, between 1983 and 1987 arrests of those under 18 for murder jumped 22.2%, for aggravated assault 18.6%, and for rape 14.6%. By the age of 16, the typical American child has witnessed through TV and movies 200,000 acts of violence, including 33,000 murders.

homicidal crimes take place within the family.[102]

According to Russian government records, in the year 1993 alone, "14,500 Russian women were murdered by their husbands. Another 56,400 were disabled or seriously injured. "Domestic violence statistics of crimes against women in England and the United States are alarming." According to Home Office research, 18 percent of homicides in England and Wales are of wives killed by their husbands, with a quarter of all recorded violent crimes blamed on domestic violence."[103]

And since children are the weakest members of the family, a greater rate of abuse is directed towards them. Child abuse is understood to cover a wide range of parental actions that result in harm being inflicted on children of all ages. The kind of abuse, however, varies with age. Infants and preschool children are most likely to suffer deliberately inflicted fractures, burns, and bruises. This is known as the battered child syndrome, firmly identified during the 1960s. Historically, reported cases of sexual abuse, ranging from molestation to incest, primarily involve male perpetrators and school-aged or adolescent female victims. More recently, however, a growing number of pre-schooled victims and male victims have been identified.[104] It has been estimated that the number of reported cases of child abuse has increased at the rate of 30 percent a year. Between 1973 and 1982 there were 1.5 million cases of child abuse; 50,000 resulted in death and 300,000 in permanent injuries.[105] Child abuse is not restricted to the U.S. In Great Britain, for example, the

---

102- Sullivan, Thompson, Wright, Gross and Spady (1980),   P. 548.
103 - **James Meek. " Moscow wakes up to the toll of violence in the home"** The Guardian, **Thursday, June 22, 1995.**
104 - Child Abuse, Microsoft (R) Encarta 96 Encyclopedia
105 - Sullivan, Thompson, Wright, Gross and Spady (1980), P. 549.

National Society for the Prevention of Cruelty to Children reports that child abuse has increased by about 70% between 1979 and 1984.[106] Based a report in The Guardian,

> In America, the number of crimes against women is rising significantly faster than any other crime. According to the latest statistics, an estimated 3-4 million women every year are battered by their husbands or the men they live with. A third of female murder victims were killed by their husbands or boyfriends."[107]

4. Rape and Sexual Harassment:

An extensive report about crime in The Epsilon issue of August 1991 reveals the magnitude of rape crimes committed in the West. The report stated that in a country like Greece whose population does not exceed 8 million, more than 10,000 reported incidents of rape were committed between 1978-1987. During 1982 alone, more than 4,000 incidents of rape were committed in Italy alone. More than 55,000 rape crimes took place in France during the 1980's. As for the United States, about 102,000 rapes have been reported.[108]

Recently, the Federal Bureau of Investigation (FBI) reported a 70% increase of crimes of forcible rape and attempted incidents of rape from the year 1970 to 1997. In 1970, only 37,990 incidents of rape were reported in comparison to 109,060 incidents in 1992 alone.[109]

---

106 - Child Abuse, Microsoft (R) Encarta 96 Encyclopedia
107 - The Gardian, Thursday, June 22, 1995.
108 - *The Phenomenon of Rape.* Epsilon, **August 4, 1991. Such incidents of rape are only those that are reported and proven in court as genuine rape. It does not include unreported incidents or those that the victims could not prove in court.**
109 - The Macmillan Visual Almanac. 1996 (PP. 370)

As it is for rape crimes, sexual harassment against employed women is on the rise too. According to the Equal Employment Opportunity Commission, the number of complaints of female employees because of sexual harassment is on the increase. In 1989, 5,603 incidents of sexual harassment complaints were filed in comparison to 12,537 in 1993.[110]

The Equal Employment Opportunity Commission stated that reported sexual harassment complaints by female employees were 10,578 cases during the year 1992. In 1993, the number increased to be 12,537 cases.[111] The problem is not only restricted to the USA, but rather a global one, especially in societies that put no restrictions in men/women relations. According to a recent report by The International Labor Organization (ILO), entitled 'Combating Sexual Harassment at Work', November 1992, many thousands of women are victims of sexual harassment at the workplace in the industrialized world every year. Between 15-30 percent of women questioned in surveys by the ILO say they have been subject to frequent, gross sexual harassment. Of all women surveyed in the United States, 42% of women reported some kind of sexual harassment. The report included countries like Australia, Austria, Denmark, France, Germany, Japan and the United Kingdom where the Labor Research Department made a survey in 1987 in which 75% of women responding to the questionnaire reported that they had undergone some form of sexual harassment in their workplaces.[112]

The Epsilon magazine continued by reporting the observations of leading psychologists, sociologists and physi-

---

110 - The Macmillan Visual Almanac. 1996 (PP. 371)
111 - The Macmillan Visual Almanac, 1996 p.37
112 - **The 1994 Information Please Almanac, InfoSoft Int'l, Inc.**

cians on the escalating incidents of rape crimes. These scientists have affirmed that this phenomenon does not occur in the animal world and is not a part of their behavior. Moreover, they linked the emergence of such a devastating problem in the West and Western-like societies where such habits and values are reinforced due to several factors among which are:

1. The media: it is one of the main factors for sensationalizing rape. T.V. films and movies show lots of violence, which include rape crimes. Most of the movies revolve around sexual and violent episodes, not just X-rated movies. Such presentations work as stimuli for imitation by the youth.

2. Intoxication has been reported as another reason, behind 37.6% of reported rapes.

3. Commercial factors were also behind the increase of rape and related crimes. The design of clothes by International Houses that show the attractive body parts of women results in many rape crimes against these women who exaggerate revealing their private body parts for the sake of public approval and attraction. A great number of rapists mentioned that the majority of their victims were of this type. Many raped women have indicated that they were raped while they were wearing exposing and attractive clothes.

4. An educational factor exemplified through mixed education where children

of both sexes are taught how to develop intimate relations with each other. Learning how to date is only one example. As a matter of fact, popular radio programs (such as the Dr. Ruth's infamous program in Canada and in the United States) are devoted to advising the public on how to establish sexual relationships.

5. The collapse of the family has forced young people at an early age to seek love outside the family. On many occasions this has led to very grave consequences. Hundreds of thousands of children in the West do not have known fathers.

6. Detaching the role of religion from the public life has brought about promiscuity.

7. Since most Western societies are built on the basis of Christian values, some inaccurate religious attitudes towards women as evil personalities might have lead to such incidents of viewing women as worthy of becoming the object of rape.[113]

8. Another reason that the scientists gave was that the law in most Western countries does not take the crime of rape

---

113 - Let's look at what canonized Saints of Christianity have said about women: Woman is the daughter of falsehood, a sentinel of Hell, the enemy of peace; through her Adam lost Paradise (St. John Damascene). Woman is the instrument, which the devil uses to gain possession of our souls (St. Cyprian).
Woman has the poison of an asp, the malice of a dragon (St. Gregory the Great).
In Ulfat Aziz-us-Ssamad. Islam and Christianity. **(I.I.F.S.O., 1982), P. 79.**

very seriously. Rapists are not punished severely, usually a mild sentence of no more than two years in prison, is given as a maximum judgment.[114]

In Hindu society, on the other hand, the life of women whose husbands have perished becomes unbearable to the extent that they have to commit suttee, a form of suicide. Gustave le Bon wrote about this aspect of the Indian society by saying:[115]

> The immolation of widows on the funeral of their husbands is not mentioned in the Shastra, but it appears that the practice had become quite common in India, for we find references to it in the accounts of Greek Chroniclers.

This disdain for females is also seen in reports by the Indian media, which report that great numbers of young girls are buried alive because the females are viewed as an economic burden to their parents.

The Times reported the one-child-only policy applied in China nowadays has led many Chinese to desire a male child and either abort female babies or kill their female toddlers or sell their older girls to mobile slave merchants. In this regard, the Chinese police have recently arrested 49 members of a gang whose job was to buy, smuggle, and sell girls all over China. As a result of this savage treatment of female children in China, the Chinese Committee for State Planning reported that the number of males is 36 million more than the number of females.[116]

The treatment of women and children in present secu-

---

114 - Epsilon, **August 4, 1991.**
115 - Gustave le Bon. Les Civilization de Inde. P. 238.
116 - In The Family, 15, September. P. 7.

The treatment of women and children in present secularist societies - whether in American, Europe, Russia, the UK, India or China - is very similar to that of the pre-Islamic society (jahiliyah). Islam came to abolish the abuse of women and children and to restore dignity to women, young and old alike.

Because of the social chaos that is taking place in many western societies, abuse is not only directed towards the weak members of the society as indicated above but rather towards those in charge of educating and disciplining. Based on a report by the Carnegie Foundation, the percentage of teachers in the U.S. who say that they have been verbally abused was 51%. As for those who have been threatened with injury was 16% but those who have been physically attacked were 7%.[117]

Away from what the law considers as rape or sexual harassment in western society, there is an alarming moral decay. In the U.S., three out of every four unmarried white women have affairs by the age of nineteen. The figure was 6% in the year 1900.[118] One out every four children is born out of the wedlock, not including millions of children who are aborted.[119] Europe is having a great resemblance to the U.S.

---

117 - The Macmilan Visual Almanac. 1996 (PP. 367)
118 - Bennett, p. 72.
119 - Bennett, p.48

Many communities all over the world imitated western ways of life aspiring for modernity and social advancements; instead they acquired their ills and wrongdoings. They were not able to acquire western technology and material prosperity.

In Canada, the number of out-of-wedlock births escalated from 4% in 1960 to 31% in 2000, from 5% to 38% in the U.K., from 6% to 36 in France.[120]

Though most examples cited belong to western countries, other non-western societies are not immune against such social ills and problems. Many communities all over the world imitated western ways of life aspiring for modernity and social advancements; instead they acquired their ills and wrongdoings. They were not able to acquire western technology and material prosperity.

The Islamic Solution

No doubt that there is a strong correlation between

---

120 - Buchanan, p. 200.

the mistreatment of women all over the world and the attitude that these cultures have towards women. Women in Islam are not looked at as the source of evil or an object of sexual gratification and abuse by men, as is the case in other cultures. Islam considers women as integral members of the family and the community. They are a source of happiness and peace.

> And of His [i.e. Allah's] signs is that He created for you from yourselves mates, which you may find tranquility in them; and He placed between you affection and mercy. Indeed, in that are signs for a people who give thought.
>
> (The Qur'an 30:21)

Islam highly praises taking care of women, both old and young. It urges fair and just treatment of women by all members of the society, whether they are daughters, wives, mothers or sisters.

> Abu Hurairah (RAA) reported that Prophet Mohammad (PBUH) said: Let him be a loser, let him be a loser, let him be a loser. Someone said, who is he, O Messenger of Allah? He said, one whose parents or one of them reached old age with him and did not enter paradise.[121]

> Jabir (RAA) said, I heard the Messenger of Allah saying: One who is deprived of kindness is deprived of goodness.[122]

> Anas bin Malik (RAA) reported that the

---

121 - Narrated by Muslim, 1758, P. 469.
122 - Narrated by Muslim, 1783, P. 469.

> Messenger of Allah (PBUH) had said:
> Whoever brings up two girls, he and I will
> come side by side in the Day of
> Judgment... .[123]

By discussing these great Islamic values, I never intend to claim that all Muslim communities adhere to these teachings and values. Many incidents of malpractices and mistreatment of women among Muslims emerge because of a very salient reason which is repelling against the authentic Islamic teaching.

The misery of aging[124] in the West does not exist in a truly practicing Muslim society. The extended family in Islam has worked effectively through history as a safe haven for its members, regardless of their sex or age. Prophet Mohammed (PBUH) said:

> Abu Hurairah (RAA) said that Prophet
> Mohammad (PBUH) had said: The
> guardian of a widow or a needy person is
> just like a person who struggles for the
> cause of Allah...[125]

---

123 - Narrated by Muslim, 1761, P. 465.
124 - America's population is aging; by the year 2030, if the current trends continue, there will be more than 50 million elderly - 1 out of every 6 Americans. (p.356) ... For some Americans, old age is the time of poverty, failing health, and loneliness - a tragic irony in an affluent country such as the United States. (P.346) ... This means that many elderly must live on incomes that are below the nationally established poverty level. (P.346) The final solution to a lonely and dissatisfying life is, of course, to engineer one's own demise. While suicide is an option at any age, the elderly make greater use of it than does any other age group. (P. 354) The above quotations are taken from Sullivan, Thompson, Wright, Gross and Spady (1980). Read what Allah says about taking care of elderly parents in 17: 23- 25.
125 - Narrated by Muslim, 1767, P. 466.

> Anas Ibn Malik (RAA) reported that he heard Prophet Mohammad (PBUH) saying, He who would like that his sustenance should be expanded and his age be lengthened should he join the tie of kinship.[126]

The mixing of exposed women and men according to the data collected by The Epsilon was a major factor in the escalating rate of rape and of battered women. The fact that Islam has prohibited unrestricted mingling between men and women helps to prevent rape crimes in a practicing Muslim society. The rule of modesty applies to men as well as women. A brazen stare by a man at a woman (or even at a man) is a breach of refined manners. Where sex is concerned, modesty is not only good form- it is not only to guard the weaker sex, but also to guard the spiritual good of the stronger sex.[127]

> Say to the believing men that they should lower their gaze and guard their private parts. That is purer for them. Verily, God is Familiar with all that they do. And say to the believing women that they should lower their gaze and guard their private parts and not display their beauty [and adornment], except that which must ordinarily appear thereof, and that they should draw their head-covers over their chests and not display their beauty except to their husbands, their fathers, their husbands' fathers, their sons, their husbands' sons,

---

126 - Narrated by Muslim, 1762, P. 465.
127 - A comment by the translator, A. Yusuf Ali.

their brothers, their brothers' sons, their sisters' sons, their women, what their right hands possess [i.e., slaves] or those male attendants without physical desire, or small children who are not yet aware of women's privacy. And they should not stamp their feet to make known what they conceal of their adornment. And turn, all of you, O believers, to God in repentance that you may succeed.

(The Qur'an 24:30, 31)

The New York Times published, in May 1993, a report which was entitled Separation Is Better.[128] The report was written by Susan Ostrich who herself was a graduate of one of the few women's colleges in the U.S. It was a shock to most Americans to find that girls in female colleges achieve better academically than their counterparts at mixed colleges. She supported her claim with the following statistics:

1. 80% of girls at female only colleges study science and math for four years, in comparison to two years of study in the mixed colleges.

2. Female school students achieve higher GPA than the girls in mixed schools. This leads a higher number of female students to be admitted to universities. In fact, more PhD's were acquired by such female students.

3. According to Fortune Magazine one third of the female members in the boards of trustees in the largest 1000 American

---

128 - The Family. **August, 1994, 14, P. 7.**

companies are graduates of female only colleges. To realize the significance of this number, we need to know that graduates of female only colleges make only 4% of the number of female college students graduating every year.

4. 43% of female professors with PhDs in math and 50% of female professors with PhDs in engineering were graduates of female only colleges.

This is further evidence from the Western world itself that lends support to the validity and applicability of Islamic principles as universal laws guiding or regulating human behavior. The Indian politician and reporter, Kofhi Laljapa, concluded:

No other religion but Islam has the ability to solve the problems of modern life. Islam is indeed unique for that...[129]

Separation between men and women is adapted by The Pentagon as a solution to many problems including sexual harassment, without given credit to Islam as the system of life that is propagating this practice to maintain morality and social peace and security. Nevertheless, Prince Charles has emphasized the great contributions Islam can provide the west with to overcome their most serious moral and social problems, during a number of his speeches on Islam and the West.

William Cohen, the American Secretary of Defense, announced the first phase of a comprehensive plan to maintain a reasonable level of morality among the male and female soldiers. The plan stressed the importance of con-

---

129 - **Emad Khalil**. They Said About Islam, **1994, in *The Islamic Future*, 27, May 1994. P. 12.**

structing permanent partitions to separate male and female soldiers in the current mixed buildings. This is only a temporary solution until newly separate buildings are constructed. The Navy also issued a number of strict instructions that prohibit the presence of female and male navy officers behind closed doors. These instructions were presented as rules that should be respected by all soldiers, especially on board Navy ships. The Defense Secretary emphasized that the rationale behind such measures was to provide a reasonable level of privacy and security for members of the difference sectors of Defense. Among these new regulations, the restriction of sleeping while wearing underwear or naked and those doors should be tightly locked during sleeping hours. They also forbid watching pornographic films in the presence of female soldiers, and imposed clearly detailed regulations regarding the type of clothes to be worn when swimming or when sun bathing.[130]

The question that we raise here is this: why are such regulations that many would look at as radical and anti-modernization imposed by the most modern country in the world? The answer is very simple: sexual harassment has reached an unbelievably alarming level and has become a threat to national security and morality. Thousands of complaints of sexual harassment by female employees rang an alarming bell.

The guidelines of Islam provide the only solution for criminal problems such as alcoholism, drug addiction, abuse of women and children, which are ravaging the world today. When western influences have encroached into a Muslim society, crime has spiraled, but where the reverse has happened--Islamic values manifesting themselves in Western

---

130 - The Family, June 1998, Issue No. 59, P.3

societies--crime has declined. In 1992 there were 847,271 prisoners in the U.S., an increase of 7% from 1991 and a whopping 168% increase from 1980. At the same time, the violent crime rate rose 27%.[131]

A 1994 Gallup Poll indicated that 80% of Americans favor the death penalty for convicted murderers.[132] Capital punishment is permitted in 38 states. In addition, some 60 crimes are subject to the federal death penalty. About 3,000 U.S. prisoners are currently on death row.[133] Capital punishment was suspended in the U.S. from 1967-1977, but was then restored. Should not one conclude that the moral fate of the world depends on the spread of Islam? Such dramatic change in the attitude of the majority of Americans toward the application of the death penalty against vicious criminals is a strong indicator of the tendency of moving toward workable solutions to the ills of our societies as explained by Islam.   ●

---

131 - Bureau of Justice Statistics (PP. 393)
132 - Bureau of Justice Statistics (PP. 390)
133 - Bureau of Justice Statistics (PP. 390)

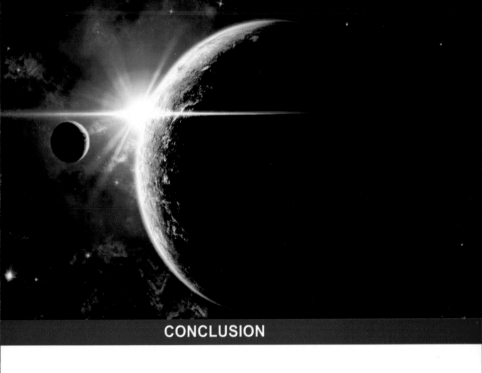

CONCLUSION

After surveying some of the major existing religious and secular systems, the probability for their application and acceptability is extremely remote and unproductive; exactly as it was with such old World Orders as Hinduism, Dark Ages theology, colonialism, communism and modern capitalism. That is because of a number of reasons:

> a. They failed to meet all the prerequisite conditions discussed in previous sections of this book: tolerance, equality, solving pressing problems or encouraging science and advancement for the good of humanity, not for its destruction.
>
> b. Their inherent nature of egocentricity and exclusiveness.
>
> c. Their historical record of focusing on

self-interest while overlooking other
nation's interests.

To understand the spirit of Islam is to understand the
very essence of humanity. More than a religion, Islam is a
complete and comprehensive way of life leading to a bal-
anced way of living. Islam brings civilization and happiness
to man. Islamic principles and teachings can provide realis-
tic, fair and objective solutions to the prevention of individual,
familial, social and international problems, which are threat-
ening the existence of human communities throughout the
world. As a Muslim famous scholar wrote:

> A spiritual belief that does not   deal with
> social behavior, economic relations and
> international organizations is as erroneous
> as the social doctrine that does not
> consider spiritual belief, morality and
> behavior. Such social doctrines are
> abortive attempts incapable of total human
> guidance or of achieving any coherence
> or accord among human beings.
>
> Both the individual and the society are in
> dire need of a belief that accommodates
> and directs all   their vital activities towards
> construction and growth. When the
> individual and society adopt such a belief
> and apply it to life, humanity can
> accomplish seemingly miraculous
> achievements, which can only occur when
> man unites himself with the Eternal Power
> that channels his personality-potential in
> the right direction.
>
> History has shown that Islam is unique in
> its ability to provide guidance for the entire

range of human activity. It does not
separate spiritual and secular life as
unrelated entities.[134]

Islam integrates all domains of human life, just like the
different systems in the human body integrate to provide a
complete human being. If one system does not work prop-
erly, it is bound to affect the whole body. Likewise, Islam
proposes systems of laws that integrate all parts of human
society to bring happiness and peace to all its members.
There is no other way or system that urges the active worship of God in its general and most comprehensive sense
other than Islam. For example, Islam teaches that Muslims
should fast for a month every year (Ramadan) in order to
acquire piety and self-discipline and to develop awareness
of the needs and problems of others who are starving or in
desperate need of food. Such an awareness of the needs of
others is not enough on its own. Therefore, zakah is pre-
scribed to be distributed among the segments of society
that are in need of individual and communal assistance.

In the words of Prince Charles "… Islam can teach us
today a way of understanding and living in a world which Christianity itself is poorer for having lost. At the hart of Islam is its
preservation of an integral view of the universe. Islam refuses
to separate man and nature, religion and science, mind and
matter, and has preserved a metaphysical and unified view of
ourselves and the world around us.… But the west gradually
lost this integrated vision of the world with Copernicus and
Descartes and the coming of the scientific revolution."[135]

---

134 - **Sayed Qutb.** Islam and Universal Peace. **American Trust Publication, Indianapolis. 1977. P. 3.**
135 - **Prince Charles, " Islam and the West."** Arab News, **October 27,
1993. In R. Hill Addulsalam.** Women's Ideal Liberation. **Abul-Qasim
Publishing House: Jeddah, pp. 41-3.**

A very important concept of universality in Islam is that of the ummah (only partially translatable as nation). Ummah transcends all limitations implied by the term nation by encompassing all people regardless of race, color, or sex. Allah emphasizes this great Islamic principle in the Qur'an:

> Mankind was one community and Allah sent Prophets with glad tidings and warnings, and with them He sent the Scripture in truth to judge between people in matters wherein they differed. And only those to whom (the Scripture) was given differed concerning it after clear proofs had come unto them through hatred, one to another. Then Allah by His Leave guided those who believed to the truth of that wherein they differed. And Allah guides whom He wills to a Straight Path.
>
> (The Qur'an 2:213)

Moreover, Islam has a unique understanding of the concept of Ummah. Ummah is the field for knowledge, ethics, government and positivism. Ummah in Islam is a system in which people integrate, even if they belong to different ideological systems. It is a system of universal justice and peace that accommodates everyone who believes in freedom of thinking and in calling people to the truth, whether they are individuals or communities.

Indeed, Ummah in Islam is an apparatus which is more advanced than that developed by the West, the U.N., or those apparatuses established by the American-European bloc merely to bring about a new world order, but which in reality often are geared only to maintain Western control over Third World human and material resources.

Prophet Mohammad (PBUH) proposed a constitution

for the city of Madinah during the first days of his emigration from Makkah. He included the rights of both Jews and Christians, thereby safeguarding their freedom and beliefs. History has never known a constitution that represented minorities as this constitution of the Islamic state did. Ummah as an Islamic concept will, Allah willing, bring the advent of universal peace as well as an internal social system. Ummah is the field ground for civilization to take place.[136] Such an Ummah can be integrated and united, if it takes its doctrines, constitutions, morals, values and the whole perspective of life from the same united source: belief in the only true God. This is known as the concept of Tawheed (pure monotheism).

The value systems of Western societies will continue to collapse, since they are built on shifting grounds. The Daily Mail of London reported the revolt by women against the values prevailing in Britain: British women seek new morality in Islam, says the heading in its inside-page report written by its religious affairs senior correspondent Lesley Thomas.[137] According to the report, this is not the case of British women who are favoring Islam. Thousands of British women are becoming Muslims in a trend that baffles feminists and causes concern to Christians. The report continues to disclose that of the estimated 10,000 British converts to Islam over the past decade; most are single, educated women, doctors, college lecturers and lawyers. The educated in the West are beginning to see that the full life is found only in Islam, the universal religion.

And what about the present day Muslim world? Unfortunately, some educated Muslims now pay only lip service to Islam. They think that Islam is a slogan to be raised or a

136 - **Isma'il al- Faruqi.** Jawhar al-hadharah al-Islamiyyah. **P. 14.**
137 - Daily Mail, December 2, 1993, P.39

What about the present day Muslim world? Unfortunately, some educated Muslims now pay only lip service to Islam. They think that Islam is a slogan to be raised or a word to be uttered. Islam is a complete way of life that should pervade all spheres of human existence.

word to be uttered. Islam is a complete way of life that should pervade all spheres of human existence. Allah dislikes those who brag about things that they do not practice. When humankind's deeds are not commensurate with words, conduct is odious in the sight of Allah.

> O you who have believed! Why do you say that which you do not do? Great is the hatred in the sight of Allah that you say that which you do not do.

(The Qur'an 61:2,3)

May Allah permit the Muslim World to be certain that Islam provides a complete and comprehensive way of life. Islam creates harmony between the mind, the soul and the body in a marvelous way that can never be achieved through any other system. The need for Islam emerges from humanity's search for a constitution that provides guidance and satisfaction in all spheres of life. It is a code of life that is not limited to partial needs, but rather a way of life that penetrates all barriers to interact with peoples' needs in this life and beyond. It is the way of life where there is no discrimination between what is sacred and what is secular.

Islam is unique among the religions and civilizations the world has known. In contrast to the other religions of the world, Islam defines religion itself as the very business of life, the very matter of space-time, the very process of history, and the gift of God. All these work together to constitute Islam.[138]

Islam is a divine guidance wherein humans of all nations, colors and tongues feel linked to a Supreme Power and Supreme Justice. Its teachings are intact and authentic. It is the only way to happiness, dignity, and universal peace. Islam is so unique in its method for solving the problems of humanity that I can say with confidence that the twenty-first century will be the century of Islam.

The everlasting miracle of Islam, The Qur'an, is a standing challenge to the intellect of all peoples at all times. In Islam's four abiding principles - equality, tolerance, promotion of sciences, and solution to the world's problems - its universality asserts itself. It calls to all humankind, if only humankind will listen.

(The Qur'an 4:82)

> Then, do they not reflect upon the Qur'an?
> If it had been from [any] other than Allah
> they would have found within it much
> contradiction.

In fact, adoption of such universal Islamic principles and their acceptance as a frame of reference for establishing a New World Order is partially, if not totally, contingent on how Muslims, themselves, view and apply its injunctions in changing their behavior individually and collectively while interacting with one another or with the rest of the world com-

---

138 - **Dr. Isma'il al- Farouqi.** Tawheed and its Influence on Thought and Life. **International Islamic Publishing House, Riyadh. 1404. P. 98.**

munity. Also, a successful acceptance by the world community of Islamic principles as a potential solution to the numerously increasing unimaginable problems of today's world, depends on the rest of the world community's willingness to give a sympathetic ear to Islam and objectively study its merits for solving the life-threatening   problems which humanity is confronting nowadays. Sir George Bernard Show, the renowned Irish writer, saliently expressed his view about Islam by writing:

> If any religion had the chance of ruling over England- nay Europe - within the next hundred years, it could be Islam.

The question that would be raised: Why would a great European writer of Shaw's caliber make this comment about Islam? He simply stated:

> I have always held the religion of Muhammad in high esteem because of its wonderful vitality. It is the only religion which appears to me to possess that assimilating capacity to the changing phase of existence which can make itself appeal to every age. I have studied him - the wonderful man - and in my opinion far from being an anti-Christ, he must be called the Savior of Humanity.
>
> I believe that if a man like him were to assume the dictatorship of the modern world he would succeed in solving its problems in a way that would bring it the much needed peace and happiness: I have prophesied about the faith of Muhammad that would be acceptable to the Europe of tomorrow as it is beginning

to be acceptable to the Europe of today.[139]

All worldly systems and ideological theories are temporarily bound and are having great flaws. Only the most authentic and the pristine teachings of God can safeguard the interest of humanity. The author holds the firm conviction that existing ideologies and unauthentic dogmas can never appeal to human needs nor respond to their pressing questions. Islam has proven to be singular in the purity of its eternal teachings and universal appeal that time does not outdate. Nonetheless, nobody can claim that Muslims fully abide by its teachings at all times and places. There were many Muslim practices that Islam does not approve of. Blame should fall on those Muslims, not on Islam. It should not be an excuse for non-Muslims to study Islam in its original and authentic sources and accept the challenge it poses for any equal in what it asserts and calls for. It would be disastrous to humanity, if major world influential political and military powers continue their war of deception and propaganda against Islam. In the end of this ongoing research, it would be unreasonable to claim that the four conditions for universality are exclusive. Other characteristics of universality like authenticity, applicability and comprehensiveness to encompass all aspects of life require further study. ●

139 - Sir George Bernard Shaw in "The Genuine Islam," Vol. 1, No. 8, 1936–in http://web.ionsys.com/~remedy/Islam%20and %20the%20Prophet%20God.htm

REFERENCES

Abddulsalam, R. Hill. Women's Ideal Liberation. Abul-Qasim Publishing House: Jeddah.

Abercrombie, Thomas J. When the Moors Ruled Spain. National Geographic, July 1988.

Al- Faruqi, Isma'il. Jawher al-hadharah al-Islamiyyah.

Al- Farouqi, Isma'il. Tawheed and its Influence on Thought and Life. I.I.F.S.O. 1403.

Al-Maeena, Khalid. *Victims of Indian's religious apartheid.* Arab News, Nov. 29, 1994. P. 10.

Al-Qaradawi, Yusuf. Non-Muslims in the Islamic Society. American Trust Publication, Indianapolis, 1985.

Aziz-us-Ssamad, Ulfat. Islam and Christianity. (I.I.F.S.O., 1982).

Bammate, Haidar. Muslim Contribution to Civilization. American Trust Publications, 1962.

Bayhaqi and Bazzaar.

Barsamian, David and Noam Chomsky. Propaganda and the Public Mind. South End Press: Cambridge, 2001.

Buchanan, Patrick J. The Death of the West. St. Martin's Press: New York, 2002.

Chambers, Carl D., Inciardi, James A. and Siegal, Harvey A. Chemical Coping: A Report on Legal Drug Use in the United States. **Spectrum Publications, Inc., New York. 1975.**

Charles, M. Apercu historique des methodes en geometrie. **(Historical Outline of Geometrical Methods).**

Church, George J. *The Other Arms Race.* Time Magazine, **Feb. 6, 1989.**

Esposito, John L. Islam and Christianity Fact to Face: An old conflict and prospects for a new ending. Common well. **January 31st, 1997**

Draper, J. W. History of the Conflict between Religion and Science. **London. 1927.**

Family, **Vol. 14. 14 August, 1994.**

Federal Bureau of Investigation, Uniform Crime Reports, **1979 (Washington, D.C.: U.S. Government Printing Office, 1980).**

Gergen. David . American Missed Opportunities. Foreign Affairs, **1993.**

Gibbon, B. The Decline and Fall of the Roman Empire VI, **1823**

Hill, Jim and Cheadle, Rand. The Bible Tells Me So. **Anchor Books/Doubleday: New York, 1996.**

Hitti, Philip K. Precis dHistoire des Arabes. **(Short History of the Arabs). Payot, Paris,1950.**

Hanbal, Imam Ahmed Ibn. Musnad.

Hunke, Sigrid. Allah ist ganz anders. **SKd Bavaria Verlag & Handel Gmbh: Munchen**

Huntington, Samuel. **Clash of Civilizations.** Foreign Affairs. **Summer, 1993**

Islam In America **(video). The Christian Science Monitor Publishing Society, Boston, Mass. 1992.**

Izetbegovic, Alija A. Islam between East and West. **American Trust Publications:** **Indianapolis.1989, (2nd edition)**

Khalil, Emad. They Said About Islam. The Islamic Future, **27, May 1994.**

Lea, H. C. 1901. The Moriscos of Spain.

Le Bon, Gustave. Les Civilization de IInde.

Le Bon, Gustave. The Arab Civilization. **(tr. Adel Zueiter).**

Mannle, Henry W. and Hirschel, J. David. Fundamentals of Criminology. **Delmar Publishing Inc. Albany, New York, 1982.**

Meek, James. "Moscow wakes up to the toll of violence in the home." The Guardian, **Thursday, June 22, 1995.**

Miller, Gary. The Amazing Qur'an. **Abul-Qasim Publishing House.**

Neill, Stephen. A History of Christian Missions. **Penguin Books Ltd., New York, 1977,**

New York Times, **August 5,1985.**

Petkept , Robert C. and Macacaba, R. L. *Food and Healthcare as Means for Muslim Evangelism.* **In Don M.McCurry (ed.)** The Gospel and Islam: A 1978 Compendium.

Phillipson, Robert. Linguistic Imperialism. **(Oxford University Press, 1992), 119.**

Pike, Theodore W., in his book Israel Our Duty... Our Dilemma. **Big Sky Press, 1984.**

Population Division, Department of Economics and Social Affairs, United Nations Secretariat, Replacement Migration: Is It a Solution to Declining and Aging Population? **March 21, 2000**

Prince Charles, "Islam and the West." Arab News, **October 27, 1993.**

Qutb, Muhammad. *Islam and the Crisis of the Modern World.* Islam its Meaning and Message. **Khurshid Ahmed. The Islamic Foundation, London. 1980.**

Qutb, Sayed. Islam and Universal Peace. **American Trust Publication, Indianapolis. 1977.**

Ramakrishna Rao, K.S. Mohammad: The Prophet of Islam. **Al-Furqan Agency. 1989.**

Sullivan, Thompson, Wright, Gross and Spady. Social Problems: Divergent Perspectives. **(John Wiley & Sons, New York), 1980.**

Sunday. **August 28, 1994.**

The American Institute of Gerontology, Information on Aging **(Wayne State University / University of Michigan,**

no. 10, October 1,1976).

The Holy Bible. **The Gidons International in the British Isles, Western House, George Street, Lutterworth, Leics. LE17 4EE.**

The Jewish Encyclopedia. **(eds.) Cyrus Adler, Isidore Singer. New York, London: Funk-Wagnalls, 1901-1906.**

The Islamic Magazine, **The Qur'an radio station 16/2/1415.**

The National Geographic, **April 1983.**

The New Grolier Electronic Encyclopedia, **1991 edition.**

The Phenomenon of Rape. The Epsilon, **August 4, 1991.**

The President's Commission on Law Enforcement and the Administration of Justice, The Challenge of Crime in a Free Society **(Washington, D.C.: U.S. Government Printing Office, 1967).**

Toutah, Khalil and Shehadeh, Bolous. Jerusalem's: History and Guide. **Jerusalem, 1840.**

Van der Werff, Lyle L. Christian Missions to Muslims. **William Carey Library, California. 1977**